GOD IS A
NEW LANGUAGE

Dom Sebastian Moore

GOD IS A
NEW LANGUAGE

WESTMINSTER, MARYLAND
The Newman Press

First published in 1967 by
The Newman Press
Westminster, Maryland 21157
© 1967 Sebastian Moore
Printed in Great Britain by Billing & Sons Limited,
Guildford and London, Nihil Obstat: Ralph Russell,
OSB, STD. Imprimatur: B. C. Butler, Abb. Pres., 12th
May 1966. Nihil Obstat: John M. T. Barton. Impri-
matur: Christopher Butler, V.G., Westminster,
4th January, 1967.

IN MEMORY OF LUKE
WHO GAVE A SHOVE

CONTENTS

PREFACE

The first part of this book is reprinted, with acknowledgments, from past articles. It reflects a mood of sharp discontent with current Catholic attitudes. It shows the way I was thinking until quite recently when the centre of the discontent shifted dramatically. The new centre was my own mind where, I suddenly came to see, the basic theological concepts with which I had been working had never really been worked out. There seemed to be considerable evidence that they had not been worked out either, as I now saw they had to be, by the generality of theologians, a fact which accounts for the sectarian quality of even the better theological writing. For when a theological notion has not been fully realized and made to hold its own in a man's honestly accepted experience of himself and others, it has to be protected from the rude winds of human interplay. It is very hard indeed to find theological writing that does not take place within a mental citadel which is a sort of invisible continuation of a now vanished Christendom. In that world, the question 'What do you mean, man?' is not heard in a disturbing way. By a mutually accepted convention, Christians, who normally deal in stocks and shares and politics and love and friendship, talk together about salvation, the coming of God, the love of God, and the love of neighbour, and so forth. In this game they do not ask 'What does it all mean really?' because they do not need to. They know the rules. They know the language. And it is the old language, a dead language. It is not less dead when it is used as a stick to beat the backs of bishops than when it is used by bishops. And so the search for understanding and a new language takes us into Part Two.

This middle section is exploratory and so, unsystematic. The pattern that emerges is, however, a simple one, and it may help the reader if we give it at once in its stark outlines.

The consciousness of a man in its lazy and habitual state is neighbourless, deathless, and Godless. It is encapsulated. The sense of his own reality, enforced with habit and the training for the battle of life, heavily prevails over the fact of existence which enmeshes him in the cosmos and makes him a problem to himself. But the message of salvation is couched precisely in these terms of neighbour, death, and God. It announces an encounter with God in a mystery of death issuing in a new community that is the place of that encounter. It implies, and demands for its real appropriation, a breaking up of the hard shell of the habitual ego. Yet it is perfectly possible to remain fundamentally encased and still think and talk of God, of death, and of my neighbour, and mean something by those terms. This talk is what I call the old language. Quantitatively it prevails over what little live religious language there is, and shapes the Christian mind. Even first-class theologians presume it and operate within it. Operate intelligently and critically, exploding old shibboleths, but still within it. Liturgical and catechetical revisionists make it more interesting, but still accept the matrix in which religious terms are formed. A point is reached where it is felt that to question the matrix is to doubt the Christian faith itself: and this is precisely the point where this questioning becomes the very condition of Christian survival. For the question 'Do I believe in the Resurrection?' is really the question 'Have I died?'

The only order of composition in this exploratory section is this. First the pattern suggested itself, and then from day to day different religious problems occurred to me and I wrote about them as I now knew I had to. And so there came under review the way we think of God, the vagaries of Christian tradition, the mind of the theologian, you, what Jesus was really on about, natural theology and the Teilhard bit, the prevalent habit of 'starting with God', how a man is 'recognized' not merely in his own society but in the whole scheme of things, and so on. All this is unsystematic, and I don't see how it could be otherwise. How can one decide in what order to recover a sense of reality?

There is a further and greater difficulty about this section. It is necessarily an attack on my own habitual unreality of mind, and one man's unreality of mind is not the same as another's. The whole struggle towards the light takes place in the world of images, and images are personal. It may never have occurred to you, for instance, to regard the world as a stage on which you significantly move. Why on earth should you follow me in an attempt to get *off* the stage? On the other hand, when communication does take place at these levels it is a far more exact and fruitful communication than is achieved when they are not attempted. In addition to this, I am convinced that there is coming to birth in our time a new facility for this kind of communication. Are we not acquiring a sort of 'lived anthropology' in which it is possible to speak at once for oneself and for man? It has recently been suggested that the question of Christian belief, hitherto posed in the more obviously public terms of rational argument, may be showing itself to be a crisis of poetry, so that the question becomes 'is there anything really and whole-heartedly to *celebrate*?' It is surely high time that theological writing got beamed on to this kind of question and to the sort of mind-work its consideration requires. So that's my apologia for section two.

Section Three follows chronologically on from section Two. I like to think it is a lot clearer and more tough-minded.

Relatively I have emerged from the fog and am throwing my weight about. The pattern of exploration has become a more or less operable structure. People say to me, 'Your "Catholic neurosis" stuff is very clear. It's this other stuff that's so baffling.' I dare to hope that this tortuous self-exploration has led me to a point where I can once again speak clearly, this time in terms that are rather closer to the real problem that lurks in all of us. For that is not a problem of bishops and nuns and 'the laity' and Church polity in this country, although it is only when it has been tackled that we shall be able to give all that business the right kind of shove. What we want is a *Christian* revolution, and a Christian revolution can only come from a Christian mind. And a Christian mind is one that spontaneously gives to such statements as 'he humbled himself, taking the form of a slave' an excitingly more than ethical sense. A Christian mind is one for whom these flaming statements are the place of an astonished self-recognition.

Finally, my original text has been drastically pruned. Originally the argument pursued in each chapter was thickly interspersed with corroborative remarks appealing to literature, drama and the events of the day. A young colleague pointed out to me that these luxuriant digressions would distract the reader unfamiliar with my line of argument. For me they corroborate the line taken. But the main task is to make clear what that line is, and this is not helped by a network of allusions. He therefore set to work to cut out most of the allusive paragraphs, and this gives an impoverished but far more clearly vertebrate text. I'm sure he's right, and I conclude this introduction by thanking Dom Peter Harvey for applying a youthful, ruthless and consistent blue pencil.

And that's about it.

God is a new language
the clasp of your brother's hand made articulate
in death, a risen Body.

Otherwise

God is a dead word.

PART ONE

Discontent

I

A Catholic
Neurosis?[1]

THE SUBJECT OF THIS ESSAY IS A DELICATE ONE. I want only to express a conviction that has grown on me in recent years: that one encounters among Catholics certain ways of behaving in the exchanges of social life: that these ways of behaving can be understood in the light of a certain hypothesis: that this hypothesis is that of a neurosis found in Catholics at the present time. My plan is to give a random list of the phenomena, then to suggest what is the root of the trouble.

To begin with, let it be clear that the case for a Catholic neurosis cannot be scientifically established. It will always be possible to reduce the phenomena listed to other causes, or even to deny their existence. The following suggestion is therefore only in the realm of hypothesis. It is offered only on the understanding that self-criticism is a good thing, that the difficulty often is to know *how* to criticize oneself relevantly, and that therefore any suggestion may be welcome.

1. First published in the *Clergy Review*, November 1961.

Here, then, is the list. A tendency on the part of us priests to be allergic to frank discussion on matters which are at once important and personal, ranging from sex to real difficulties with the faith. The effect is that people encounter, at a certain point, a barrier which is not so much the limit of orthodoxy as the limit of the priest's willingness to talk as a man. They feel that 'he wouldn't say that if he were free'; and 'free' here does not mean 'uncommitted to the faith and practice of the Church' but, well perhaps 'free *in* that faith and practice, made free *by* that faith and practice'. More often than not, the preferred alternative is to keep right off important subjects and to cultivate a sort of impersonal *bonhomie* – a tendency especially marked in clerical gatherings.

A certain unsatisfactoriness encountered in religious institutions by laymen in their employ. Whether the laymen are right in saying 'I shouldn't be treated that way by a secular body' is not really the point. The point is that they do say it, often, and that they may be right, so that we have here a hint which, in the terms of this article, I cannot afford to ignore. Often they are struck by an absence of straightness in the conduct of affairs. When something needs correcting, the person concerned is not told, but others are, and in general things are handled obliquely. Occasionally the layman encounters something like hysteria. I heard of someone the other day, employed in a large school run by religious. There were complaints about what was considered excessive frankness in his teaching on sex. His interview with the head-master was perfectly amicable, but at the end of it the head-master said to him, 'I believe Fr X has something to say to you.' Fr X then appeared and, in the presence of the head-master, accused the man, in most intemperate language, of corrupting the young, poisoning the wells, etc.!

A tendency for young Catholics to remain strangely immature. A priest friend of mine asked some Catholic girls at the university for their ideas about marriage, and the unanimous reply was: 'I don't want to marry a Catholic. Catholic boys are so immature.' He then got exactly the same reply from Catholic boys about Catholic girls!

A tendency to blow up simple things to tragic dimensions. Pamela, aged twelve, writes to a friend at another school. In the course of a chatty letter about Elvis Presley, Adam Faith, and the musicals she saw last holidays, she remarks that life at school is 'deathlike', always the same faces, how she envies her friend being at a day-school, etc. The letter is read by the Reverend Mother, who sends it to Pamela's mother with a covering letter in which she wonders whether Pamela's attitude is 'sincere' or 'merely a pose'. If it is a pose, she says, it is surely a most unpleasing one. The letter is supposed to show 'a most undesirable trait' in the girl's character, an attitude that is very hurting in view of the efforts made to entertain the girls.

Now, what all these examples show is this. Something seems to be inhibiting a direct and simple approach to the routine problems that life puts up. What I am going to suggest is that this inhibiting factor is liable to be a feature of the Catholic mind.

Every man needs some ideas, some principles for interpreting life to him and for guiding him in its conduct. But there needs to be some *balance* between this ideal structure and the unique life which it is guiding. A man needs to 'realize' his ideas, to feed into them a personal discovery of their meaning and usefulness. Now, with the Catholic, this ideal structure is most imposing. It is the creation of Christian faith working in great and holy minds, bringing forth their best insights. From the meditations of Augustine, from the speculations of Aquinas, and from numberless other sources, there has been built up this great body of objective truth. The effect is peculiarly accumulative in the Church, whose law it is that every significant Christian insight feeds and increases a common mind. And whether or not your individual Catholic is overtly aware of all that he carries, he does carry it. At moments he will surprise his non-Catholic friend by showing an astounding *certainty* about life and death and God and after-death, problems about which the greatest minds have anguished without conclusion. Now, this effortless certainty is a wonderful thing, and I have sometimes pointed to it, while instructing a convert, as showing the real meaning of infallibility. Still, if I am right in saying there must be some balance between a man's ideal structure and his life as experienced, there is going to be a serious imbalance in the case of the Catholic. Between him and what *he* feels and, fumblingly, thinks about life – 'life' meaning girls, money, marriage, fun and drudgery – there comes what great and noble souls have thought about it, twice-born souls who have seen the true perspectives and made the consequent sacrifice. So he oscillates between two standards. This oscillation is not the same thing as the tension between good and evil, between the dictates of conscience and the importunities of the flesh. It is a division of the mind rather than of the will. It is better described as a neurosis than as a straight spiritual conflict. And it is the Catholic ideal structure, getting between the individual and his rudimentary common sense, that tends to inhibit a commonsense approach to the problems of daily living.

The neurosis will be more active in those whose manner of life commits them more closely to the Church, and that is why the symptoms I have listed are those shown by us religious. This is a hard saying and takes no account of the numberless souls who have grown, in religious and priestly life, into fine men and women. But I'm not writing about them. I'm not even writing about the redeeming feature (in the strong theological sense) in our own lives. I'm writing about the other side of the picture. I want to understand why it is that a religious community may fail, sometimes to an alarming degree, to develop the natural virtues of community life. After all, it is this sort of thing that our layman in religious employ finds himself up against. He misses in his employers a type of straight dealing and sanity that is more easily found among men not embarrassed by supernatural awareness. And I want us priests to ask ourselves: Am I such a small man that I cannot worthily represent to others an infallible and inflexible authority? And let us avoid the stop-thought that immediately offers itself: of course no one is *worthy*.

This division to which the Catholic soul is liable can have many effects. The principal of these is apathy, or what a seminary professor of my acquaintance once referred to as 'Catholic pessimism'. He was speaking of the seminary itself, where the ideal structure is built up in all its imposing coherence. The effect of being continually exposed to the truth which is doing one no good is distressing to the soul. There can even result a kind of unbelief, an exhaustion of the spirit, which is all the worse for being partly unconscious. In this connection we ought to look up what the old masters have to tell us about accidie, which may be loosely rendered as 'spiritual bloodymindedness'.

And outside the seminary! The young teenagers who go straight from a Catholic school into the factory, what of them, what is in their minds, what *can* be there? What relation will there be between the formulas they have learned and the life they are beginning to discover?

Well, we might take one example, a common one: the young man struggling with masturbation. Masturbation is radically an immature practice, and the proper function of grace just here is to help him to outgrow a boyish habit. Probably the habit survives, as a sort of pocket of immaturity, in a life that is otherwise developing well enough: so that our young man is a *man* at his drawing-board or on the shop floor, and a small boy in his bedroom – *and in the confessional*. That is the point. Somehow, the way he thinks about his struggle religiously arrests it at its juvenile stage. Nor is it difficult to see why this is. His religion tells him that what he does is a mortal sin – worthy of eternal damnation and so presumably a rather adult affair. A good counsellor would tell him it is an immaturity. These two considerations do not easily combine. So he will choose to continue the struggle, week by week, exclusively in religious terms, and so preclude the natural light that he really needs. This phenomenon is relevant to our subject. It is an instance of how the Catholic ideal structure can be too much for the individual – in this case the full analysis of an act in terms of human destiny has prevented its being understood in its personal context. It is not *himself* that the young man has brought into the confessional, but a timid Catholic soul, a soul that will continue to give the same sort of account of itself at thirty, forty and sixty when, as an important and responsible businessman, he will be confessing disobedience. And thus it is that Catholic religion can have, *materialiter*, the same effect on the young as the vast mass of salacious literature available on all bookstalls – for this is nothing but a commercial racket for keeping us all at the adolescent stage.

What is the remedy for all this? First of all, perhaps we should not be too hasty to blame ourselves but should recognize the problem as something bigger than we could have created by our imprudence and inertia. There is a sense in which the Catholic Church has never really grappled with 'modern man' as he emerged from the break-up of medieval culture. The Reformation was a movement that started within the Church, lost its head, left the Church, and provoked in the Church a powerful reaction which culminated in the Counter-Reformation – the analogy with counterrevolution is not to be ignored. The Catholic of today is still waiting to enjoy that 'sanity in religion' which is to be found, mixed with heresy, in the reformed churches. The problem has roots deep in history, and so there is no easy solution. Once this is realized, we may proceed to make a few modest suggestions.

We must come to see what are the factors which accentuate the *rigidity* of the Catholic ideal structure, which prevents it from being assimilated, which cause its truth to drown the soul rather than water it. I think immediately of two: polemics and the fossilization of the liturgy.

Polemics. The habit of thinking of Catholicism as something which we have got and the others haven't got has the curious effect of making us less conscious of what we really *have* got. Somehow the very strength which Catholic truth develops in conflict tends to alienate it from the soul. One can end up by presenting Catholic faith as the answer to a question that one has ceased to ask oneself. It is encouraging to know that the faith one is trying to give to our teenagers can hold its own against Bertrand Russell, but to give it to them one must be able to listen rather than to propound, to listen and be surprised as the soul of man speaks its needs in new accents.

Fossilization of the liturgy. A priest wants to be *with* his people. Above all he wants to be with them in the celebration of God's mysteries. He doesn't want Mass to accentuate the gap between the Catholic Thing and the Catholic man, with himself on the Thing-side of the gap. If one allows oneself to think, it is really nerve-racking to turn one's back on a congregation of dockers, seamen and teenagers, and proclaim (for all to hear, as the rubrics insist!) 'Os iusti meditabitur sapientiam'. He might even have such rebellious thoughts as 'I'm tired of saying Mass. I want to take a service – which will be the Mass of course!' Indeed the present rubrics illustrate well the tendency of the last centuries to take the Catholic Thing away from life and wrap it up into a tidy parcel containing all the essentials except what is essential for *us*. For the present Mass is an abstract of the Mass–liturgy, flattening out its many dimensions into a single plain surface which only the expert can penetrate.

It looks as though the liturgical section of the coming Council [this was written in 1961] is envisaging radical reform, and, in general, it is clear that this is an age of fresh discovery, in which Catholic truth will manifest its life-giving rather than its conceptual properties. The object of this article is to stimulate a generous and open-minded response to these changes by pinpointing a long-standing *malaise*. I believe that there is such a *malaise*, and I want to keep my eye squarely on it and not get diverted into all the individual things that want reforming. There are moments when one seems to see so many things – the lapidary Latin declaimed to a pop-record congregation, the outlandish things one hears in the confessional from people one knows to be normal if a little dim, the twists and turns of politics in a religious house, the self-torture of nuns, the waspishness of Reverend Mothers – as parts of a single lunacy. There's very little real malice in the most unpleasant symptoms – the petty tyrannies, the roundabout approach to administrative problems, etc. It's just that we're such children. It is our faith that makes us so – and it shouldn't. It should make us men and women, marked with the Cross and sensing the Resurrection.

But it may be that the picture I have drawn, in which so many things are seen as symptoms of a neurosis, is itself neurotic. In which case, perhaps I have demonstrated the existence of the Catholic neurosis – by succumbing to it!

2

Out of
this World[1]

FOUR YEARS AGO MY ARTICLE "A CATHOLIC NEURO-
sis?" had a spirited and varied reception. It laid itself wide
open to the charge of being a set of random impressions
selected to make a point, and this, according to the socio-
logists, is the unforgivable sin, though I doubt whether this
was the only reason why the article was disliked. And now,
after reading Monica Lawlor's book,[2] I feel that it was just
as well for the 'Catholic mind' that I was not competent to
subject it to her kind of sociological analysis. For the picture
that emerges from her methodical and impeccably well-
mannered analysis is far more devastating than what I presented in an erratic and not always charitable squib.

The young Catholics – teacher trainees, seminarians,
religious, those in fact who are now being formed in order
that they may in turn form the next generations – fit placidly

1. First published in the *Clergy Review*, August 1965
2. *Out of this World* by Monica Lawlor. (Sheed & Ward, Stagbooks.
15s.)

into the 'religious type' of the Allport–Vernon–Lindzey Study of Values test.

The overwhelming overall impression from the results obtained from the various tests is that these young Catholics have their priorities right but have very little idea of, or concern about, how this right order works out in practice. They are content to say that *without* the love of God one cannot love one's neighbour, but are strangely unconcerned and incurious as to how the love of God flows into the love of one's neighbour. There is little evidence of the realization, so strongly marked in St John's great epistle, that the absence of a positive concern for others is the surest indication that God is not loved at all. In other words, our young guinea-pigs are sound on the 'essential' proposition: no love of God, no true love of neighbour, but strangely unalive to the 'existential' proposition: no love of neighbour, no love of God. And note that with this latter proposition, the love of neighbour really is primary and irreducible, in such wise that the only way of finding out whether I love my neighbour is to ask myself whether I ever do anything for him. It is invalid to say 'of course I love him, because I love God, of *that* I am sure'. For St John's whole point is that *that* is just what one can't be sure of.

Miss Lawlor's summary of results obtained from the questionnaire on 'how does the good Christian behave?' is as follows:

Well, there is the Good Christian, concerned about prayer and God and individual moral but not material improvement; rejecting the puritan virtues rather firmly, little concerned with the world, and finally rather in favour of the Bomb. The Good Christian is seen as one who is concerned with God and prayer and with following the example of Christ, but he does not set much store by things like going to evening classes, being kind to animals, giving up the Bomb or helping local charities. He is theocentric, concerned with his own conscience, but not concerned with the personal virtues and social involvements that characterize much of the English way of life at its best (pp. 62–3).

Again:

In fact this rather vague dimension (the religious as presented by Allport, Vernon and Lindzey and getting top priority in the young Catholic answers) could well be summed up in terms of spirituality, reverence, and a religious interpretation of the physical world. What it clearly lacks is any sense of religion as visiting the sick and imprisoned or helping widows in their affliction – though it could well be described as unstained by the world, from which it would indeed appear to be very remote. It is a very Other Worldly orientation (pp. 49–50).

Another valuable observation:

This figure (obtained from secondary-modern schoolgirls) shows the point we have already noted of the greater importance attached to the liturgy by the schoolgirls. These children also find community responsibility and loving their neighbour as important as private religion. They live far less out of the world in spite of being several years younger and presumably less intelligent than the student group (p. 76).

This last observation counterpoints interestingly, I think, with the fact that the lapsation rate is much lower among grammar school products. This is regularly taken to mean that the more intelligent you are the less difficulty you have with religion, and the apologist is keen to make a point here. But it could also indicate that a less down-to-earth approach to life is more congenial to religion as we conceive and teach it. As Miss Lawlor puts it: 'Successful mentalization and interiorization may preserve the faith of the better educated, but it could be that other members of the Church are paying the price which such disinvolvement entails' (p. 80).

Finally, I cannot ignore a precious detail unearthed by the author – the child who does not go to communion because she is frightened of not finding her place when she gets back. Suddenly one sees the whole thing – the rows of worshippers wearing that fixed post-communion look, the peculiar form of public assembly that contrives to inhibit all the ordinary responses, and in the middle of it all, the lost child. How long will it be, I wonder, before new liturgical customs succeed in thawing us out at Mass and ending the anomaly of God presenting himself to us precisely in our social, mutually aware condition, and us responding in mutually conceded privacy?

And now I should like to try to get a theological angle on the spiritual impoverishment to which Miss Lawlor is pointing.

In the first place, God is love. If, then, the God who *is* love becomes available to man who is a conscious subject capable of loving, how are we to conceive of man the lover's part in this affair? It is essentially receptive. There is not here the initiative that is present when one man loves another. Man as subject has been touched, awakened, enlarged, inspired, quickened (etc., etc., etc.!) by a love that eternally is and pre-exists him. The love that God has *for* him has been given by God *to* him, and is now *in* him. At this point the rational theologian has understood, correctly, that we cannot speak of God's love, which is infinite, becoming itself an act of finite man. And so we must describe man's end of the affair as a finite participation in the infinite love that God is. This participation is the love that is in man, the love that man, renewed, has. Is this love a *love for God?* Surely, since it is unthinkable that man should become a conscious participant in God's love without his act being a conscious response to the infinite love that has touched him, and the only response to love is love. But we must be very careful how we think of God as the object of this love in man. For if I say I love someone, I am not saying anything about my relations with any *other* person. Whereas if I say 'I love God' within the framework of the Christian Revelation, I *am* formally and *per se* making a statement about myself in any and every situation where love could arise, that is, in any and every contact with another. For the Christian statement 'I love God' is the statement that I am touched by the God who *is* love and so am constituted 'a loving person', a person reshaped by essential love and so made loving in the totality of my human, social situation. Thus 'not to love someone' is quite simply, to be without the love of God.

Now a teaching which stresses 'loving God' is in danger of becoming forgetful of this Christian meaning of the phrase and of understanding it in terms of the ordinary statement 'I love X', a statement that refers to me and X and no one and nothing else. It is surely of profound significance that hardly anywhere in the New Testament is the concept of 'love for God' formally invoked. Of the places I can recall, one (and that, I think, the only one in the gospels) is a dominical quotation from the Old Law, another a reference to someone who says he loves God and is lying, followed by the axiom that he who loves God must love his brother (1 John 4: 20 ff.).

The whole structure appears in the following text from 1 John:

> Dear friends, let us love one another, because love is from God. Everyone who loves is a child of God and knows God, but the unloving know nothing of God. For God is love; and his love was disclosed to us in this, that he sent his only Son into the world to bring us life. The love I speak of is not our love for God, but the love he showed to us in sending his Son as the remedy for the defilement of our sins. If God thus loved us, dear friends, we in turn are bound to love one another. Though God has never been seen by any man, God himself dwells in us if we love one another; his love is brought to perfection within us (1 John 4: 7–12, NEB).

The striking thing about this text is that love for God is

formally said to be not here the point. To shift any emphasis on to our love for God would be to upset the balance of the thought, the whole point of which is that 'the unloving know nothing of God'. 'Unloving' must have the widest possible sense if the thought is to work.

Is there not a profound weakness in our tradition that consists in having been voluble just where the New Testament is reticent, in having formalized as an attitude to God (and indeed a very 'formal' attitude) what was originally the Christian attitude that is '*of* God' and that commits us to the whole world of his making and predilection? And is it not just this weakness that we find faithfully reproduced in the answers to Miss Lawlor's questionnaires?

There's something awfully peculiar about this 'Catholic God'. Just in so far as he is a being whose cultivation makes us less interested in the world we live in, he is not God but an idol of our own making, the personification of our desire to keep ourselves to ourselves. Now there's nothing peculiar about an idol. Our museums are full of them.

But the power of this idol is derived from the undoubted truth that God exists and is wholly separate from this world. It is an absolutely strangling combination of truth and falsehood. I found myself saying the other day to a lapsed Catholic – a woman – 'You've got a dead God inside you and you got him from your Catholic upbringing.' Though thoroughly lapsed, she still has a very 'Catholic' notion of the God she has left, and this makes a return to the living God extraordinarily difficult for her.

And of course once God has been got into this position, such that the cultivation of his company has become an activity that can stand completely on its own as a 'religious interest', an activity judged 'more important' than those human commitments wherein alone the love of God truly shows itself, then God is reduced to the finite level. For he then competes with other people for our attention in such wise that attention given to him is taken away from them, exactly as a man's business will suffer if he gives free rein to a consuming interest in music or pictures. For all its apparent transcendentalism, the attitude pinpointed by Miss Lawlor is precisely a denial of God's transcendence. It is also to be noted that the initiative of God in Christian love is not really an integral part of this attitude. It is the attitude of people who have chosen God, not of people whom God has chosen. And it is all of a piece with this attitude that in it Christ appears not as the sign and pledge of God's transformation of us in love but as the perfect moral example, which is how he appears over and over again in Miss Lawlor's 'answers' – which, by the way, are quite unspecific as to what we *learn* from this example.

If there is one word that describes this attitude, it is 'thin'. First of all it is humanly thin, rarefied. As against the famous Latin tag, there are only too many human things that it thinks alien to it. Next, it is thin spiritually. Though it is 'mystical' in so far as it shares the off-beat mystic's indifference to sublunary matters, it has none of the vitality of mysticism. It might be called a legalized mysticism, an anomaly parallelled by the idolized transcendent God who is its object. Finally, it is thin theologically. It is represented by a thin line going up from 'the soul' to 'God', as against the broad stream of God's love coming to us in Christ and possessing us with a Spirit of unity.

A word in conclusion. Miss Lawlor's book will inevitably invite reserves. But it would be tragic if they resulted in the cumulative impression that the book is not, after all, telling us something about ourselves that we shall ignore at our peril, something the continued ignoring of which will make the 'vocations crisis' a chronic ill and will show itself in that progressive alienation of the young of which the vocations

B

crisis is only a symptom. We have to ask ourselves: even if she is over-sanguine in her faith in this or that test, even if she betrays a certain bias, still, is she not in the main telling us what we know to be the truth about ourselves? The question is really an appeal to ourselves, to our honesty, to our conscience, though perhaps to a sector of the latter that does not get much exercise.

PART TWO

The Search
for Understanding

Introducing
the Exploration

I START MY EXPLORATION WITH A SEARCH FOR A concept of God. What I mean by a concept here will become clear only as the work proceeds. A concept, basically, is an aid for thought. It is an arrangement of the material that enables the thought to be rightly conceived and to grow. What happens in your mind is profoundly mysterious, even to yourself. What we call communication is the throwing out of hints so that your thinking may start and find its way, find your way for you.

A concept of God is peculiar. It is of its nature not definitive. Really it is confined to arranging the materials in the hope that a certain liberating thought, a thought that *is* liberation, may take place. For the Christian, these materials are real happenings in this world. They are a certain life, talk, death and resurrection. They are all the things that are happening to man today and to each man in his own little today. It is these human materials universal in their human relevance that I shall be pushing around.

The whole approach may seem unfamiliar. But I dare to

hope that what I am talking about will gradually come to
assume in your mind the shape of something absurdly
familiar; hitherto, incredibly, unknown. It is your life that
matters, that life from which you have persistently escaped
into worlds of our making: that life which Christ claims for
his own. Our life is polarized between sex and death, the
ecstasy whence we come and the dissolution to which we go.
Polarized? Yes, in moments of consciousness; but for the most
part, for most of the time, and in terms of most of the ideas
we receive from society to live by, we are in an interim that
knows nothing of these two things. This is the human lie.
This is our godlessness. This is the invalidity in our religion.
Religion, for most of the religious, has little to do with the
God who places us between the poles of sex and death and
calls us there into the fire and light of his presence. On the
contrary, the God of religion is a God we have adopted,
invented, in relationship to whom we can work off at small
cost to ourselves the sense of dependence that in its native
form is unbearable.

There *must* come at last the real Christian poet, the man
who will conceive in the fire of the Spirit the whole human
predicament. Who will speak the original word of flesh in
which our doom and our salvation are written.

Do people never *think* when they read the writing on the
lavatory wall? Yes, absurdly, that is where our Mane, Thecel,
Phares is written. It is the measure of our lostness that we
relegate the direct statement of our origin (and, in some
cultures, of our end as well – four-letter words for death!) to
the public convenience. Has not all our religious culture so
far been a refinement of our civilized self-awareness, a further
refinement of our self-refinement? In other words, has the
Redemption ever succeeded in being more than a scientific
description, a correct formula for a correlation that has never
been humanly absorbed?

When he comes, the real Christian poet, as opposed to the poets who have been charmed or deeply moved by the Christian thing as by a beautiful thing in our life, the glow in romanesque or gothic or mystical baroque: when he comes, we shall see the strangest people drawn towards the Church, as it was in the beginning.

At present we lack not only the Christian poet but the poet of our time. The word of our time is spoken only by the arid iconoclasts who, lacking the fire of the Spirit and the self-knowledge that glows in that fire, can only replace the images with abstractions such as Event and Commitment. Is it over-ambitious in me to want to call the breakers and the preservers of images into a common Christian vision and charity?

I

A Concept of God
for our Time

WHAT IS MOST LACKING TODAY, BOTH IN THE world and in the Church to which the world at least sometimes looks for light, is an adequate concept of God. By this I mean not, of course, a concept adequate to the reality of God, but a concept whereby we could understand that in God alone can man hope to find fulfilment. The *fact* that God alone can satisfy is often stated: but the *how* of it, that specific human flourishing that can only be in God, is never made clear. And the continuous statement of the fact without explanation causes a steady debasement in the value and meaningfulness of the statement. Living in a large city, I find that the garish announcements of salvation that daily stare at me from the posters outside our blackened churches induce in me a mood of unbelief. This is increasingly experienced by the sensitive preacher when he comes out with the time-honoured and time-worn phrases ('God alone . . . in God alone'). How can he tell people – how can he even tell himself – that this being called God, who has nothing to do with life as we experience it, is the centre of all our striving? There was a time when God had a lot to do with human life and experience, and it is from this that our image of God, of the God who cares, is still taken. The concept of God with which we still operate is the focus of a religious experience that was once vital and is now being immobilized in lifeless jargon.

It is only in the writings of the great mystics that we read excitingly of God. And even this excitement is offered to us not as people immersed in the experience and tensions of today, but as individuals who have turned away from the world – the world of today in which alone God can write his will for us, his claim upon us. And most of us fare even worse than the privileged readers of the mystics. To most of us is offered a 'God' who is not only remote but whom we have no real reason in ourselves to wish near.

My appeal will be to human experience – what else is there to appeal to? But I shall consider human experience not only in depth – the depth of solitary mystical vision and the depth in personal relations – but also in its full extension – the wide-spread human fact that has in it much more than experience of persons in solitude and in love.

And in this wider context, I hope to show a specific form of human awakening and flourishing that could only be the response to a transcendent influence. The flourishing and the influence in question is that documented in the scriptures and witnessed to by the Church. There is no question here of an 'argument for the existence of God from human experience'. What I am trying to find out is simply this: how should we, today, the inheritors of so much religious tradition and so much religious bric-a-brac, *think of God* if we want to hear relevantly and fruitfully, and preach to the world, the word that is written in scripture and lives in the Church?

By way of a guideline for what follows, consider that no one has really offered us a concept of God such that, in its light, we may *understand* the undoubted theological fact that the supernatural love for God and the supernatural love for people is one same love. Two loves build two cities. But in the City of God there is but one love.

The Concept

Clearly the only way we *can* think of God as a person is with *some* sort of reference to persons as we know them. The attempt adequately to conceive God in this reference goes through four stages.

1. Thinking of the human person as a conscious knowing, willing, and doing/making subject, we say that God is such a subject with all limitations removed. This is conception at the level of the *Penny Catechism*.

2. We may think of the person not in solitary terms as above, but in relational terms: as someone we encounter and love. We then think of our relationship with God as being *like* a relationship with a human person. This is the conception-level of the average *spiritual book*.

3. We may go on and say that our personal relationships not only tell us about God, as in 2, but actually mediate him to us: that he somehow underpins them: that we meet him *in* our relationships, not merely through a comparison *with* our relationships. At this stage, our language about God becomes vague. He is not so much a person as the essence of *the personal*, encountered in those moments when a personal relationship is experienced in great depth. This is the level of the Bishop of Woolwich's '*Honest to God*' (S.C.M. Press, 1963).

4. The fourth way is far more radical, and marks a break with the assumptions of the first three. The most important of these assumptions is that 'personality' is a given, fixed, and simply known reality.

'Person' is classically defined as the individual substance of rational nature. This definition tells us little or nothing about what we nowadays understand as personality. I do not wish to place on a pedestal 'our modern notions'. I merely state that *if* we are asking such questions as 'What's a person like?' we cannot expect answers from the classical definition. And we *are* asking just such questions when we seek an image of God based on our experience of persons.

The 'personality' into which I am now enquiring may be loosely defined as 'the sense of oneself'. While it is true that the basic self-awareness is identical with the conscious subject, what we mean by personality is the appropriation of this self-awareness, that says 'I' and immediately confronts the problem of relating oneself to a context, the world of people and things. The 'I' with which we are concerned is the 'I' that is consciously 'not *like*' the things around me and consciously 'other than' the persons around me.

Now this personality has to be slowly *acquired*. It is not given from the start. We are in process of *becoming* persons. Built right into the core of our being is the necessity and desire of becoming someone. To become, successfully, someone is to become mature: to arrive at a convincing feeling of myself over-against others, such that my relations with others are not inhibited by an identity-crisis in myself. Those who have not achieved this are people we perceive to be awkward and define as immature.

But this notion of maturity has an in-built limit. For maturing *is* a self-limiting. It involves a mastery over those in-built urges that stem from our being originally *built in* to the bundle of existence which we have to *cope with*. Personal existence involves the consciousness that we are *in* something that we can never appropriate, for it is essentially 'the unappropriated', the non-personal that is undeniably a part of the human reality. Man must, in this sense and for this reason, be a puzzle to himself as he makes his way through the world. He is forever learning from the world a language of which he does not know the principles. This basic human agnosticism finds expression in all the human arts: tragedy, comedy, poetry, music and painting, and the avowed limitation of philosophy as a discipline of self-understanding. The root of all this is the awareness of myself over-against other people: that this is a self that I have made and had to make: that this self-making is in contradistinction to the flow of life whereby I would, I feel, flow right into other people and lose myself in the process.

And thus it is that man surrounds his sexual life with taboos, makes laws to protect himself from his neighbour, and, when he does flow into his neighbour, does so under the protective convention of romantic love or, at the limit, of tragedy. A total surrender to the flow of life is, for him, death. How much modern literature insinuates that living is impossible, 'living' meaning here a total adequacy to the flow of life all around and through our being. (Most Christians protect themselves from the precious lesson this literature contains by classing it as pornographic.) As a sign of this inbuilt human agnosticism, consider the following. The question 'Who am I?' is obviously the most searching of all questions, much more searching than 'What am I?' And yet to this profound question I can only give a trivial answer: a name given to me not by God but by the society in which I happen to live and be known.

Now I want to look at two things:

1. Man aware of himself over-against others.
2. Man thinking of himself as a person over-against God.
These two both involve a denial of reality. Be I never so alive to my brother and his needs, there is a certain rigidity, a life-denying immobility, in the image I form, and must form, of 'him and me'. To suggest, as I think Woolwich does, that in our more profound personal relations we altogether overcome

this unreality is to misunderstand the matter profoundly. But when I come to set this self-made-me against God, I formalize and hold in its pure state the lie that I cannot altogether escape in my relations with my neighbour. Now what I am going to suggest is that when God, by a free and gracious initiative, enters into a relation with me that dissolves my illusion of being a person over-against him, melts with his grace the immobility inherent in the self-made me, he dissolves in principle the *derivative* lie in my relations with others. He sets me completely in the flow of worldly existence and transforms it in the process. He brings me to the death that is inherent in my total surrender to the impersonal flow of life, and thence to a Resurrection in which *he* is truly known and *I* am con-corporate with my brethren. Thus a quite *new* sense of 'myself and others' – whose image is the Body as opposed to the confrontation of bodies – is the sign of an encounter with the self-giving God. The concept of God thus implied, although making him underpin our personal relations, has nothing vague about it, as it *must* have if I attribute ultimate reality to personal relations conceived irrespectively of the world in which they are knit. The new concept of God is intensely personal. Our relationship is now felt to depend on an initiative which is not our own.

I only wonder why I call this concept new. In fact it draws on all the basic doctrines of the Church: the profoundly felt biblical notion that man in confrontation with God is 'nothing': the cognate doctrine that our relations with God are wholly and solely originated by a divine initiative: the doctrine of death and resurrection, of grace and the refashioning of man: the identity between the love that embraces God and the love whereby the Christian loves his brother, profoundly felt in the New Testament and never totally recaptured in subsequent mystical and ascetical tradition: the doctrine of the Body of Christ: the doctrine of the Trinity which is, however, here so closely wound into the dynamic oneness of the saving God that it is barely formalized (with the corollary that it never has been formalized without some weakening of this dynamic vision). Our 'new' concept differs from the older ones precisely in that it, *and not they*, embraces all these doctrines. The 'old' concept is of a God who, *as a matter of fact*, has done all the things described by the doctrines. The 'new' concept is of a 'shape' of God presupposed by, and discerned within, the event of our salvation.

It is also called for by the age in which we live, an age preoccupied with the meaning of human existence. It is an age that can be very convincingly invited to take a new look at man, to become aware of the unsuspected foundations of that brotherhood of man which it increasingly endeavours to bring about. It is an age that is seeing a sexual revolution in which sexual passion is seen in the light of the mysterious unity that binds us all, rather than as the matter of a personal ascesis: and that is willing at the same time to be profoundly critical of its sexual revolution, as being a luxury of affluent man, guiltily averted from the wider connotations of the social fact, the needs of the hungry and the maimed. It is an age that confronts for the first time the problem of leisure, and the implication of a positive definition of this problem as opposed to the double negative (*not* being *bored*) in which it is usually articulated: an age, then, in which man is striving 'consciously to be'. It is an age to which one can convincingly say, 'Your ordinary, decent life is teetering on the edge of total meaninglessness unless you commit yourself totally to others'. It is an age in which the best formulation of the human desideratum is felt to be of its nature atheistic: an age, then, in open opposition to an idea of God that is idolatrous. It is an age which can only maintain hope with the aid of a new concept of man – and a *really* new concept of 'man totally renewed'.

But we shall not say to this age: only God can renew man.

We shall say that only a renewed man can know God. We shall present God as the root of renewal, and thus disavow, as the private luxury of socially uncommitted man, the God we have so ineptly preached.

Finally, it is an age profoundly suspicious of the attempts of Christians to modernize their doctrine and to be too ready to tell people of goodwill that they are 'Christians without knowing it'. And this we inevitably do, when we simply take over the new personal values without subjecting them to the breakdown that I have tried to suggest. Also, it is a logical age, that will not be slow to reply to the Christian modernizers: 'If we can be Christians without knowing it, what is the point of becoming knowingly Christians?'

2

God, Man
and Cosmos

BEFORE HIS COMING-OF-AGE, DURING WHAT HAS been called the intra-uterine period of the human race, man succeeded in *fixing* himself as *somebody* and the world to which he belonged as *something*. Natively, man is a to-himself unintelligible intersection of 'person' and 'nature', of experienced self and the whole bundle of existence into which the self extends, could be lost and, at death, *is* lost. The first solution of this problem is, to become absolutely convinced of one's own independent reality, and to sustain this conviction by declaring the world to which we belong to be separately and equally meaningful. Thus the world, which is in reality a process with a direction of its own which would pull men into its personal movement, becomes a *stage* on which man securely and significantly moves.

Now God is conceived of as securing, separately, man and the world-stage. He is a person who has, *of his own right*, that independence of the world that man has only by his own unacknowledged separation of himself-as-a-person from himself-as-nature. And thus you have the notion of the God-Person as differing only in degree, albeit infinitely, from the man-person. It is a part of the faith inspired by and answering to this God-concept, that man is meaningful on *his* side and the world is meaningful on *its*.

In this present world, man is going into solution. Under the pressure of his scientific achievements both speculative and devastatingly practical, he is becoming what he basically is, a baffling intersection of personal awareness and seemingly endless cosmos. He is suffering the identity-crisis that is inscribed in his very being. He no longer *asks* a question. He *is* a question.

Now with man gone into solution, the God-concept necessarily goes into solution too. The God whose very meaning was found in the meaning he gave to the world out there now completely fails to give this meaning and so is dead. The God whose very meaning was found in the assured dignity of the human person as he moved on that meaningful stage now fails to give this meaning and so is dead.

We Christians are now suffering acutely from a situation in which the new human identity-crisis is blandly met with a God who knows nothing of this crisis. The tragic irony is, that the new situation is exploited (sometimes: sometimes not even that) to show that the religious question is more single, less academic than ever before. Here, we think, is a far more convincing apologetic than we have ever before had to hand. Man is wrested out of his old domestic-universe security, made a problem to himself, set staring into the meaninglessly teeming galaxies, and *then* the apologist considers his task well and truly done. Man now is one big single question, and that the religious one. The answer? God of course! God as we have always known him. The Lord of a universe that no longer exists. The Lord who governed the sedate movement of the heavens and now ('far more wonder-provokingly', we ineptly add) controls the Big Bang.

In making this kind of response to the big new question of man, the Christian tradition is not giving of its best, or even of its substance. For the New Testament presents a God who is known *only* in the total destruction and re-creation of man of which it is the record. The New Testament does not tell us about God apart from this context of regeneration. According to its witness, God is the meaning, shining out of the very depths of man's contingency and meaninglessness. It was the dismayed apostles, hollow men for whom God was dead, who proclaimed, in accents never heard before, the Living God. They proclaimed him by being the indestructible community that sprang into being when the risen Lord appeared to his own.

In this important respect – of God's appearing *in* the dissolution of human meaning – the New Testament, far from being in another world than the man of today, can throw the definitive light on his experience. Conversely, the New Testament itself springs to life when read by post-modern man. As only a mathematician can write a history of mathematics, so only a man who has died can understand the death and resurrection that is the theme of the New Testament.

But this real meet-up between the man of today and the New Testament can only take place across the ruined monuments of the Christian world. And this is not a case for a theological scorched-earth policy. The ruins have to be understood, for they are part of the very furniture of our minds. And the new insight into God that is now available for us is importantly clarified by its contrast with the idols on which we were brought up.

The chief of these idols is the monolithic God of the medieval cosmos. This is how he came to be. In the Christ-event, and in the community that embodied that event, God was known. Known only *in* the event of man's passage from death to life, from darkness into light, he was perforce known *as* the Lord of all that was or could be. For it was part of the

Christian experience that 'the world' was no longer the alien world to which agnostic man is subject, but was concorporate with the new man as he stood before the Lord. Now, apart from this central experience, it is possible for man to have *some* knowledge, 'by the light of unaided reason', that God exists. But this knowledge, for all its reality, is of a very modest kind. It is not properly a knowledge *of God* at all. It is a knowledge *about the world*. It is the realization that the world is not self-explanatory. Even this term 'not self-explanatory' has to be understood in a rather special sense. For the 'God' to which it leads us is not an explanatory principle. This wants elaborating, but the present context is not the place for it. The point here is that in the identification, which perforce took place, between the God of Christian Revelation and the God known apart from that revelation, something of the positive and affirmative quality of the former came to inhere in the latter.

This had serious consequences. The God who is personal is properly known by us only in the Christian encounter. It is only in that encounter that we know what it *means* to say that God is personal. He is not known, apart from that eruption of the personal in the life of man, as a person one can talk *about*. But this is just what he tends to become when he is transferred to the new context of natural theology, whose whole method is rational and uncommitted, a way of talking about things in themselves apart from their effect on us.

This mistake resulted from saying, inaccurately, that our rational knowledge gives us 'only a very poor notion of what God is like'. From this it is a natural step to say that the Christian Revelation *fills out* our sketchy rational knowledge of God. The accurate description of our rational knowledge of God is that it gives us no knowledge of *him* at all, not then a knowledge that could be said to be 'filled out' by the Christian Revelation.

And once this loss of balance has taken place, the tendency is for the whole thing to swing right over. People begin to think as though this rationally known God-Person somehow *preceded* the God who shines upon us in the face of Christ Jesus. Revelation itself comes to be thought of as a series of propositions, amplifying the propositions that are the proper product of reasoning. And so you get the monolith. Le Grand Solitaire reigning in the skies and one day sending his Son on a mission of goodwill (and collection of dues!) to his distant kingdom.

Formal theology, e.g. Aquinas's *Summa Theologiae*, seems to have avoided this mistake. But formal theology was powerless to prevent the grand monarchical medieval God-image from forming and sitting over the west doors of Europe. He is a thing of rare beauty and, curiously enough, once we understand his provenance, and the battle royal whereby the Church of the Middle Age fashioned unregenerate man into a Christian civilization without wholly regenerating him, we appreciate him (the Christian Zeus) the more. But as the Ruler of the Catholic mind for all time, he must be dethroned. Our God is a consuming fire, and the fire is in our hearts. He clothes with glory the flowers of the field that are cast into the oven, and even in the nuclear oven his glory may be revealed.

Note 1: The 'Personal God' of the Gallup Polls

Since the unawakened Christian tradition still gives to the expression 'a personal God' the false meaning and associations I have been trying to pinpoint, it is not possible to say whether a man who 'does not believe in a personal God' is doing more than reacting against this spiritual irrelevance. So much for Gallup polls.

Man has become a problem to himself. Now this is a big step towards truth. It might almost be called a dark night of the soul undergone by society as a whole. And the *main* modern complaint against the doctrine of a personal God is that this doctrine seems to be asking us to step back, not forward, on this spiritual journey. The way forward is towards a world mysteriously apprehended as one, in which personal values are values of growth in community, not values of independence. The way back is towards a congeries of sovereign independent entities ruled by a God who has this sovereign, solitary character to an eminent degree. The Christian faith seems to be asking men, conscious of falling apart, to pull themselves together again and, thus reassembled, to reopen communications with the Sovereign. Which is a strange message to hear from a faith whose whole substance is death and resurrection and divine grace.

Note 2: Language

A very important factor inhibiting the formation of a live God-concept is the poverty of theological language, the absence of recognized language-games other than the sedate one in which a statement is an equation.

Here is a very germane example. In conversation I once found myself saying, quite naturally (and being immediately understood), 'Of course, people are part of God'. Taken literally this is pantheism. More important, the statement taken thus is not only false but silly and boring. It wasn't what I wanted to say, and it didn't occur to the other person for a moment that it was. As intended, the statement was a straight description of the Christian life. (The freedom of language to do its job is significantly dependent on the sort of person one is talking to.)

This becomes clear when we paraphrase the statement thus: the acceptance and the care for people is an integral part of the God-business. We must then go on to recall that for scripture the God-business *is* God. God is 'our refuge, our stronghold, our strength', all those things that the analytic mind pulls apart to set 'God' on one side and 'his effects' on the other. What God is *for us* – salvation – that he *is*.

Thus my statement 'people are part of God' is not 'an inaccurate and possibly misleading way of putting things' – the correct way making a clear separation between people and God – but is only a contemporary version of the dynamic, living language in which the impact of the living God is originally documented. It is simply a matter of learning once more to talk God. There is a difference between talking something and defining it: no sane person stops in the middle of a conversation to subject what he is about to say to the canon of scientific accuracy. But we do just this when we try to talk God, with the result that we never talk him at all.

Further, the statement 'people are part of God', while being inaccurate against the scientific canon, secures a *kind* of accuracy that is very easily lost when we confine ourselves to scientific discourse. For there is a special difficulty about talking of people and God together that is best circumvented by a certain restraint in the dotting of i's and the crossing of t's. If I say, for instance, 'Loving people is an important part of loving God', I am saying something whose repetition by the press will not bring a letter from the Curia, but I allow the fatal impression to grow that God is someone and people are someones *in the same sense*. I altogether lose sight of the dynamic and inclusive character of 'God'. I continue to propagate the limited out-there 'God' from which the Christian tradition is becoming the fossil of a past age and failing to mediate the living God to people living today.

Note 3: The Trinity

Someone is bound to say: 'You are insisting on a vital

concept of God. Yet you make no mention of the very doctrine whose theme is God's life – the Trinity.' Further clarification may be achieved if I say that the Trinity, at least in our usual understanding of it, is in part the cause of the trouble. For my question, "How are we to think of God as a person?', is not clarified but fogged by the reply 'He is *three* persons'! What understanding we *can* have of God as three persons depends upon an initial opening of the mind to the simple, dynamic, enclosing and transforming concept of God that I am trying to clarify. I don't think one can work this in reverse, getting to the vital concept by considering first the Father, Son and Holy Spirit.

In saying this, I do not align myself with the 'Western' approach which goes from the One to the Three, any more than with the 'Eastern' approach which goes from the Three to the One. It is incredible that we can still play the game of contrasting these approaches, not realizing that in the centuries that stand between us and the men who first tried to hammer out the *grammar* of God the whole God-concept has gone into solution. Our problem is the different one of trying to locate our thought and talk of God in the context of our thought and talk as people living today. While *as theologians* we continue to weigh up God in the received and hallowed language of people who no longer exist, the God-problem piles up in ourselves who do exist and do not know who we are.

3

The Resurrection of
the Christian Conscience[1]

YOU ARE SOMEONE, BUT ALSO AND EQUALLY YOU
are part of *something*. Nature did not labour through all those
eons just to produce a suitable dwelling-place for your personality. She did not elaborate all those eyes and ears and
things just so that *you* could establish communications with
what you call the outside world. The human body is not a
sort of super-expensive toy. It is very misleading to call it
your body: to exist in the body means to be bound by a
thousand ties into the whole bundle of existence. This in-
binding, which is beyond our personal control, is *us* just
as much as what we call 'I' is us.

Further, even that part of our being which we call the
personal, where we are conscious of having some control, is
not to be conceived of as a sort of inner sanctuary, a cultivated
garden walled off from the wilderness outside. Our most
intimate experiences, our most direct awareness of ourselves
and others, are connected to the far-reaching human and

1. A sermon preached to the Catholic students of London University.

sub-human grid. If we became completely alive to the grid and identified ourselves with its demands, we should, I suppose, totally lose ourselves. Something like that happens at death. In life, we make a compromise. We build up our personality – at first this is largely done for us by society – as a sort of HQ, and HQ admits as much of the other side of ourselves – the instinctual, etc. – as it can cope with. And in admitting these drives, it changes their meaning, or tries to. The sex-drive, for instance, loses its meaning as a part of nature pursuing an intention *of her own*, and becomes raw material for *our* disciplining, a horse for us to break in. It doesn't really, of course. That's the lark. Although sexuality is, in part, a part of our personality, whose disciplining will enrich our personal being, it is in very large part what it always was, nature pursuing an intention of her own. And this is not to down-grade sex. On the contrary, it is to insist on the deep and wide mystery of sex and man generally. It is to insist that man is a problem to himself.

A problem, for we know ourselves as able to dispose of ourselves and so responsible for the dispositions we make: but we also know in ourselves a heavy element of fatality, in our involvement with family and in some of the attachments we form – those ones where we feel the other person in our bones, so that to withdraw from the attachment is to deny ourself. And beyond that, we have no assurance that the vast cosmos into which we are knit is arranged for our benefit. When St Paul said that for those who love God all things conspire together for good, he meant something pretty terrific and demanding by the love of God. We certainly can't paraphrase the statement: 'for those who have the good fortune to be Catholics'.

I think that Christians have no idea how agnostic man is bound to be about life's meaning and purpose, and through what pain and darkness God gives the meaning and the way.

They look out not on the universe that exists, but on a universe said by others to be humanly meaningful and friendly. They look in not to the puzzling struggling man that they are, but to the man that others have told them that they are, a soul in temporary exile from home. Who are these others? Whence do we receive these Christian spectacles through which we inspect the world and ourselves? From Christ? No, from a Christian culture that is now passing away.

Even in the post-medieval period, running from the Renaissance to an unfixable point somewhere in the last fifty years, the ancient fixed pattern of God, man and cosmos remained. It was weakened, however, because the God who ordered the now scientifically known cosmos was the God of Deism whose days were perforce numbered, and because the self that still looked securely out on this cosmos was not the Christian man but the liberal inspired by Christian ethical values, and his days were numbered. The writing on the wall was E equals mc^2, and vast new social convolutions of which we have not yet begun to take the measure or grasp the meaning.

In our day the ancient pattern is totally shattered. There is no God, in the way that a medieval man or a seventeenth-century man who hardly ever said a prayer could say with complete assurance that there was a God. Man today finds no reason to believe that the universe is meaningful or friendly. He wonders profoundly whether he *is* anyone except in his practical relation to his immediate environment. He sees no reason to restrain his sexual and other urges except reasons of practicality.

It is an age of moral bewilderment. For it is only when life as a whole is felt to be meaningful that rules of behaviour are felt to be anything more than practical dispositions at the traffic-control level. God said, 'Walk before me and be perfect'. Modern man can attach no meaning to 'walk' in that sentence. The stage has gone, and what of the great Spectator? To ignore all this, and to attribute the contemporary break-down in morals to *external* corrupting influences, such as drink, TV and modernistic parsons, who are supposedly invading a position that would otherwise hold us, is a disas-trous mistake. It involves two false premises:

1. That the ancient pattern is permanent and so still able to give to man his meaning and direction.

2. (And this is far more serious.) The equation of this ancient pattern and the meaning it gave to man's life, with the Christian message and the meaning *it* gives. And this brings us to a central paradox.

The Christian Revelation stiffened the pattern of ancient man. It endorsed the dualism of a meaningful cosmos on the one hand and a meaningful man on the other. It instructed him to find in that cosmos the materials for sacramental worship. But centrally the Christian Revelation was the most radical *dissolution* of the pattern conceivable. Its centre was not 'man knowing himself in a meaningful world', but man dissolved in death, reduced to the death that ever gave the lie to the human myth of a friendly and humanly meaningful world out there. The world is not a stage but a process in which man is engulfed and lost, and this humanly unbearable truth is the place of God's coming to us in the risen Christ. It is in death, in dissolution, that the new man comes into God's presence and loses for ever the anonymity of man. The only liturgy he knows is the liturgy in which that death is celebrated.

And thus it is that man today, just *because* he is going 'into solution', just *because* he is losing the meaning he once had, just *because* the monumenta of the Christian world seem to him irrelevant, just *because* he no longer knows who he is, is potentially nearer to the heart of the Christian thing than ever before. History has plunged him into that fluid, problematic condition of himself in which the Word of God originally apprehends and remakes him. He is without the stage-props of an earlier and less mature Christian age. He has lost his crutches. The ghastly mistake of so many Christians is to mistake this for a loss of legs.

If you want to know what it is to be dead with Christ, read St Paul. But if you want to know what it is simply to be dead, read Sartre and Camus, or any of the signs of our times in yourself or in the world. And if you don't read any of these signs, can you be sure that you are giving to the word 'dead' in 'dead with Christ' its full human weight, and not some vague mystical significance that will neither demand nor endure much thought?

It is man in solution that God acknowledges and raises up in Christ. It is not man as he would prefer to be acknowledged, decently distanced from his neighbour and from the bond of flesh that associates him in the impersonal drive of nature. It is basic man, problematic man, nameless man, man without dignity. It is man in his unmanageable mutual and world-involvement: the involvement he has to deny if he is to live on his own steam as a person. God, and only God, can take man *in* his involvement, and in so taking him he creates the new community. Is it man he takes, or is it the bundle of existence in which man is dissolved? The question is really without meaning. But the Scripture gives us a clue when it says, repeatedly, that God (and it is not referring to creation) calls man out of *nothing*. You weren't anybody till God called you.

Now the *being* into which God thus calls man is essentially a community. The impersonal mutual involvement becomes, in the risen Christ, a love between men such as the earth could never have seen before. Charity is not the denial of the flesh but its transvaluation. Every other rational love of others *is* or involves a denial of the flesh. Charity is the infallible sign of

God's presence. It is the definition of God. God is an intimacy in the flesh that otherwise is death.

It sprang into being when the risen Christ stood among the disciples, men plunged by the death of God into an *experience* of the purely human that we do not normally have at the conscious level: an experience of death that is normally the death of experience.

It is towards a fuller awareness of and commitment to this community that the Christian conscience has to be directed. Here are some directions, some marks of the Christian conscience in our time.

1. It will notice, and give new life, urgency, and meaning to the movements of love in our time. For it will be alive to that new awareness of others as our own flesh and blood, which is characteristic of an age in solution.

2. It will readily understand the so-called sexual revolution. This too is characteristic of an age in solution, in which people become newly alive to our mutual involvement. Sex, we now understand, is not so much a passion within the individual (the Greek ascetic concept) as a mutual involvement of us having an intention of its own. It is because of this that man in his sexual involvement is eloquently representative of man-in-solution, man awaiting redemption, and that Christian marriage is the symbol of regenerate man. The Christian conscience of our time will subject the sex-urge to charity – flesh-affirming and recreating charity, not to the purely self-regarding control to which we were brought up.

3. It will look with amazed recognition at much in modern literature, which shows us how unlivable life is once one really attempts to break below the surface. What it shows us is not merely *how great* is man's need of God but *what* this need is in terms of man as we know him and are him today. And this should alert us to the unreality of much of the God-talk.

4. It will beware of all attitudes that savour too much of

the world that is gone, the ostracisms, the veneration of institutions, the imposing edifices. It is not a question of 'the new at all costs', but of what exists as opposed to what no longer exists. And the attempt to restore a past order brings out unpleasant characteristics in those who engage in it. Leave resurrection to God. He knows how it's done. He raises dead men, not dead things.

5. It will, in other words, be acutely sensitive to the difference between the Christian faith and the Christian world.

6. It will be alternately amazed that anyone becomes a Christian, and that anyone doesn't.

7. It will believe in the birth of a new world.

4

How to read the Bible — Keep on your Toes

IN STATEMENTS ABOUT GOD'S COMING, LOVING US, etc., the *God-concept* has a fatal tendency to wobble idly between the totally beyond-our-reach and the within-our-reach, occupying the one position when we want to show how wonderful he is, the other when we want to show how maty he is. There has to be, in theology, a central insight accompanying the 'God-us' type statement: an insight whereby we understand that the statement does not operate with *fixed* terms, 'God', 'us', but declares a new meaning of 'us' to which 'God' is the self-introduced key. The Christian statement cannot operate with preformed, hardened terms. It uses these terms, but it puts them into solution in doing so. The 'we' to whom God comes is a we plunged back into a sort of human *materia prima* and resurrected as a Body in which he is revealed. That is the meaning of 'God loves us'.

To say 'God loves people' is to confront the whole problem of God and people, and to declare its unique and manifestly divine solution. This is what the kerygma is doing. The statement 'God so loved the world that he sent his Son, etc.' is not a statement about someone called God. Rather it is giving *the meaning* of God and challenging the theologian to conceptualize this meaning so far as he may. It is describing the transforming encounter whose place is the Christian community, the encounter in which alone God is personally known, and to which we have ever to refer for the meaning of the proposition that God is personal. To repeat the kerygma without this understanding is to imply that the two terms 'God' and 'us' describe two realities whose meaning is fixed *apart* from the statement, or at least does not receive from the statement a crucial increment. Now the 'we' thus fixed is a community of men sufficiently convinced of its own meaningfulness on the stage of this world to be able to be called into relationship with God. But in fact the human 'we' is only real and meaningful *in* the call of God. The only meaning otherwise acquired by it is mythical, and modern man has exploded that myth. In outgrowing the myth he comes potentially closer to the real call of God. Simply to repeat the kerygma to modern man without showing him the 'communication of meaningfulness' that is its substance is to invite him to reinvest himself with the myth and accept the overtures of a God himself compromised by this game of make-believe. Ironically, his sales resistance to this treatment is inspired by the very God that it is trying to put over him.

As Christians, we have to arrive at a state where our approach to people and our love of God are properly correlated and unified. That is to say, we have to get right beyond the attitude which apportions one slice of the cake to God and another to our neighbour. This Christian task *is* in practical form the theological problem of the *meaning* of person as applied to God and to my neighbour, or better, the meaning of calling God a person in statements that refer to people. The attempt to love my neighbour in the love of God is grounded not in a statement about what 'God' thinks of 'my neighbour' but in what 'God' and 'my neighbour' mean in the statement of the redeeming event and fact that brings them together. The Christian is ever asking of God, 'Who is my neighbour?' The answer he receives is the self-revelation of God.

Rule for reading the Bible

Do not break down the Bible's statements about God. When you read, for instance, that God is our refuge or our place of pasture, or our life, do not understand such descriptions as applied 'improperly' to one whose *proper* description is as a being separate from his remaking and calling. The usual thing is to say that 'God who helps us' is called, improperly, 'God our help'. 'God who' statements are taken to be 'proper', while 'God something' statements are taken to be improper and are resolved back into 'God who' statements. Thus to call God a King, a Warrior, is considered *more* proper than to call him a place, and this because our paradigm is always the separate and unavowedly circumscribed being. Thus we resurrect for our security the God whose death is our salvation.

C

5

You

YOU ARE INDEED A PROBLEM. YOU DON'T WANT TO be messed around, and how right you are. And yet, whenever you succeed in establishing your independence, you are miserable. For then you feel you do want to be interfered with, and very profoundly. You want to be entered, possessed. You want to belong.

You accept what is called society. For society is a compromise between your desire to be untampered with and your desire to belong. And the law of society is – Law. Under its protection, people are kept at exactly the right distance from each other.

You get so tired of people who tell you you are being selfish when you are only being yourself. But then you get so tired of being yourself. Though you would never admit this to those tiresome people.

In love, in the all-consuming love, all seems to be resolved. And yet here too, here especially, the human contradiction can burst upon us, so that Coleridge can write of the lover who

> Must needs express
> His love's excess
> In words of unmeant bitterness.

It is only in the romantic phase of love, when the beloved is not really *there*, that the human animal tolerates the thought of a total absorption in the other. And even here the note of guilt appears. Here is a quotation from Chateaubriand (from *Objections to Humanism*, p. 113):

> . . . sometimes I could have wished to be with you the only living creature on earth; sometimes, feeling a divine prompting which would check me in my horrible transports, I could have wished that this divinity might be annihilated, so long as, locked in your arms, I might have rolled from abyss to abyss with the ruins of God and the world.

Divine promptings? Underlying every reference to the divine, there is a certain concept of God, and the concepts vary. In this case, it is the concept of a benevolent Ruler who warns his subjects against the excesses to which they are prone. Of which more anon.

Sexual love culminates in orgasm. And orgasm often, perhaps more often than not, alienates the lovers. *Post coitum tristitia*. Is not the deepest reason for this that orgasm represents a primordial commingling of the two, from which the individual, habitually encased in his egoism, holds back?

Death nowadays has been de-religionized. It is unlikely that the thought of death will produce in you the traditional religious anxiety. But it will puzzle you, and if you are one of the intense types, the puzzle will take the form of anguish. Speaking for myself – and in the matter of death one can only speak for oneself – I find myself thinking as follows in an aeroplane. Here am I, so deeply habituated to a world of planning and execution that I cannot realistically envisage its termination, forced to recognize that just now that world depends on those jet-engines. Imagination toys with the sudden plunge, the impossibly brief, drastic, and undirected revision of all possible plans, and then dozes off. It is not for nothing that I think of a *world* depending on those beautiful engines. For it is characteristic of the intensely felt reality of the self, that I take the whole world into myself. Nothing is so real to me as myself: but the world too is real, so that I promote it to my own reality-status. Though I would never admit to anything so preposterous, I live on the assumption that the end of me would be the end of the world.

That the world should suddenly and casually end seems absurd. But equally absurd is the assumption that *my* world is *the* world. And so death appears to me as the cancelling-out of absurdity by absurdity.

The equivocal fight for personal independence, the agon of sexual love, the thought of death – these are the crisis-situations. The humanists tell us they should not be pushed. They insist that we Christians are pushing them because we want to squeeze out the religious solution from the riddle of the universe. They point out that by far the greater part of human living is exempt from this type of anguish, and that a sane and mature individual comes to accept, without any detriment to his personal growth, the social formula: indeed that those who insist that the social formula is only a compromise, unworthy of their aspiration, tend to get nothing done and to remain immature. Alex Comfort puts this point of view very well. 'We are getting kinder and more comprehending in proportion to our rejection of religion and other short cuts which professed to have all the answers.'

But there are indications today that the personal problem is appearing over a disturbingly wider area of the human scene. The scientists who worked on the first atom bomb found themselves faced with a situation in which the ancient and honoured rules whereby the individual has hitherto discharged his limited obligations to society were thrown violently into question by a loyalty hitherto without practical, and therefore moral meaning: a loyalty to the whole human race viewed concretely, concretely destructible, a loyalty that could not be described without cynicism as involving a *partial* obligation. And surely this is only the prognosis of a problem that is going to involve us all and demand of us, in the words of Paul VI to the United Nations, that we 'come to think of man in a new way'.

The central contradiction of man is that man *as a person* is at once absolute and limited. Absolute, and so, it seems, independent. Limited, and so dependent. It is because of this that he rightly resents interference and validly desires it. It is because of this that love is for him a struggle between surrender and resistance. It is because of this that death bewilders him. It is because of this that the vast social problems of today are becoming unmanageable even within the limits set by a previous age: for the human contradiction has itself broken down those limits, so that even the decent life is becoming problematic as the adventurous life always was.

A generation ago, Christians would have had little hesitation in offering the religious solution to man in this predicament. It was the period when C. S. Lewis could turn the tables on the unbeliever in brilliant debate, and make him, and not the believer, the butt of public amusement, at least at the University level. It was the period when Christian apologists could point to the high statistics of religious practice at the universities and then predict that the spread of education would mean the spread of religious conviction. And then there was comforting old Jung to assure us that nearly all psychological problems were really religious problems.

But now one hears, on all sides, of a Christian 'loss of nerve'. I don't know why Christians have lost their nerve, but I think I know why they ought to have.

Let's take this problem of man: this feeling of having absolute status in an unmanageable form, a feeling aggravated by the fact that today the whole universe seems to insist on

our personal insignificance. Now the usual religious answer
is: certainly the human person is absolute, irreducible, and
the subject of inalienable rights. If he is to be himself subject,
this can only be to one who enjoys personal being not in a
limited way but absolutely. It is only by self-dedication to
such a being that man can, consistently with his own absolute
status, adequately acknowledge the dependence that he feels
to be part of his nature.

The big difficulty with this, which I shall state in rather
abstract terms because this is how my mind works, is felt,
I am sure, by all sorts of people who would not be able to be
so articulate about it. And the difficulty is almost essentially
inarticulate: that this business of 'personal absoluteness' is
inextricably intertwined into our finite situation, albeit it is
the latter that calls it into question. The whole knot of personality is so tight that it is impossible realistically to conceive
of the absoluteness of personality 'in the pure state' and so
predicate it of God. It is no accident that in his *Summa Theologiae* Aquinas never does this.

In any case, in practice the 'Christian solution' as above
described has the effect of setting up a supreme person who is
essentially the *enlargement* of the 'knotted' human person: who
has absolute power 'by right', being untrammelled by the
conditions that limit our personal existence. Thus the 'solution'
is legalistic. Above arrogant man (and there is a tendency at
this point for the human condition to be described in moralistic and emotive rather than in its own tragic terms) there is
the Lord who rules him: who holds over him the sort of
curbing dominion that society exercises, but by right. And
when the Christian religion tries to thaw out this somewhat
forbidding picture by saying that this God *loves* us, it thereby
fatally underlines that very human-writ-large characteristic
of the personal God that is the cause of the trouble.

And so you have: man, left in his unresolved, 'knotted'

condition, and, over him, a God who is man-writ-large, a monarch who, of his pure munificence, has deigned to enter into relations with him.

And thus the malaise which modern man feels in himself is made worse by being transplanted into a ruling God. Both God and man have, in this picture, a solidity, a fixity, that makes the one unbelievable and the other despairing of redemption.

Redemption indeed there is in the Christian scheme. But it is normally seen not as a significant release from man's actual and experienced plight, but from a condition whose origin and meaning are sought in the further improbability of a sin on the part of the first human pair. Between the fixed 'God' and the fixed 'man' you have a whole host of things requisite to the relation between them. This picture is not significantly altered by merely asserting the love of God for man as the *raison d'être* of these 'Catholic Things'. The plenary statement of that love must, I believe, overtly consider the 'crisis of personality' that man is and is discovering himself more and more to be. And this involves a new way of thinking. We have to set the saving God and problematic man in a new and creative relation. Our guide for this is the radical dissolution and resurrection of man in which the saving God is, according to the witness of scripture, encountered. We have to find salvation in the very *concept* of God and not merely as an operation attributed to a God independently conceived. We have to reverse the direction according to which a hardened man-concept has led to an even more hardened God-concept: learning to look beyond the *problematic* man-concept to an inclusive, dynamic, and saving meaning. We have to hear anew, deeply and with the ear of our revolutionary time, the words of the prophet: 'I will take the heart of stone out of the midst of you, and put in you a heart of flesh.' We have to reach a way of thinking about the all-renewing God, for which the *problem* of relating the love of God to the love of our neighbour will be profoundly and instinctively felt to be a false problem: posed in terms of a God who does not exist and a neighbour seen with the dull eye of custom.

The only writer I know of who really attempts to renew the concept of God and to relate it excitingly to a new type of human association is Teilhard de Chardin. It is surely symptomatic of the terrible hardening of the Christian mind that this new idea had to be presented under cover of a scientific myth – the convergence of individuals on 'point-Omega'. (Cf. *The Phenomenon of Man* for Teilhard's progress of man via 'concentration' and 'decentration' to 'surcentration'.) The fantastic appeal of Teilhard should be a challenge to theologians to produce in primary theological coin what he has suggested in the language of a secondary discipline fired with poetry. We must bring into creative relation the upheavals of the present time and the upheaval that took place in Palestine 2,000 years ago when the stone was rolled away.

Finally, the concept of God, the notion on which people work and base their values, is never the product of speculation alone or even primarily. The forces that have gone into the creation of the 'hardened' God-concept have been the forces of self-control rather than of love. If it is true – and surely there is much truth in it – that these forces have prevailed in the Church over the values of love, then we should expect this imbalance to show itself in the God-concept. The hardened God-concept is the projection of knotted man's attempt to curb the forces latent in his problematic personality, as opposed to the radical Christian surrender of this personality to the transforming force of the Spirit. God has been the supreme lawgiver rather than the saving power. And it is but a superficial renewal which is content to attribute to the God thus conceived the qualities of love and mercy. A genuine

Christian renewal in moral and spiritual life must chain-reaction in to the very heart of theology, where God shows his face and we are saved.

There is nothing new in all this. It is simply a question of paying renewed attention to the New Testament grammar, according to which 'salvation' is (a) found in, and shown forth by, a new community of man (b) identified with the saving God: 'He bloweth with his Spirit and the waters flow'.

6

Jesus's Teaching

THERE IS AN ASPECT OF CHRIST'S TEACHING THAT has not received due attention. Much has been said on the *content* of the teaching, both ethical and dogmatic. The recent emphasis on the eschatological dimension has been most fruitful in enabling us to unify the dogmatic content, organized as it is now seen to be round Jesus's announcement that the time of God's definitive entry into human history is come. And this new principle of interpretation in its turn gives a new edge to the moral aspect of the teaching, which is now seen to be not so much laying down timeless ethical norms as describing the behaviour appropriate to this 'fulness of time'.

But, as I say, there is still another aspect to be considered. I mean the attempt to recreate in our imagination the teaching of Jesus as *event*. What I have in mind is suggested by a question such as: What is Jesus trying to *do* to his hearers? What, essentially, is the difference of vision and outlook between him and them, and so what is the nature of the communication being attempted? What is the barrier against which he is using all his resources as a teacher? Consider together the following characteristics of Christ's teaching: the frequent use of irony: the especially violent criticism of the professionally religious with phrases like 'straining for the gnat and swallowing a camel' highlighting, by their manifest absurdity, the absurdity of the literal pharisaic mentality: the scandalous and quite unqualified preference for rogues and prostitutes: the setting up of the child as the embodiment of his teaching: the frequent allusion to the way things happen in this world, shockingly given as an example to follow – the unjust steward, the complaint that the un-profitable servant could at least have made some profit by usury, the recommendation to settle with your adversary out of court, 'because you know what "justice" will cost you!'

Dare we attempt to say what is the underlying aim of Christ's use of all those resources of friendly teasing, irony, cajolement, and earthy realism which we don't seem to have noticed? (cf. *The Humour of Christ*, by Elton Trueblood. Darton, Longman & Todd, 1965). In other words, what is the basic human situation that Christ is trying to break into and break down?

To begin with, it is the basic human condition. Anyone who has begun to understand the gospels will recognize himself, time and again, in the formal religiosity of the pharisee, so easily scandalized, so ready to misunderstand, and in the obtuseness of the disciples – in other words, in the two areas where the element of misunderstanding receives a heavy, constant, and deliberate stress. When, for instance, Peter asks, 'How often should I pardon my brother – seven times?' and receives the weary answer 'O seventy times seven times', do we not hear ourselves asking the priest for 'a definite answer' as to whether such-and-such is a sin or not?

What is this human condition as we meet it in the gospels?

Its essence lies in the fact that when man tries to be religious, he forgets to live. And this is perhaps the most radical fact about religious man: from it stems the stupid literal-mindedness of the religious, the desire to have from their religion a cut-and-dried solution that life itself can never give, the inhumanity and pomposity of religious leaders, the arrogance of theologians who were prepared, not so long ago, to torture people into their way of thinking, the anti-life atmosphere so easily generated in church, the endless hypocrisy which is all the worse for being sincere. Jesus turns to these poor benighted 'children of light' that we are, and commends the unjust steward who at least showed common sense.

There seems to be a certain *immobility* about religious people, a failure to be quite alive and aware, which goes to the very root of fallen man. This inability to be at once religious and real is the sign of man's alienation from God: he is compelled to put God into a special category removed from real life and so characterized by the unreality, the fixedness, of 'religion'. God formed man in his own image. But man *re*forms God in *his* own *religious* image. And in obedience to this God, man goes through the paces of religious observance, meticulously, one by one, clocking up his merits, correcting his faults, oblivious of the teeming world in which he is being hurried along to death – for is not death, too, taken care of by religion?

Into this air-tight world of religious man, Christ breaks with the force of a total, single, earth-knowing Godliness. Not surprisingly, it earned him crucifixion. Very surprisingly, yet completely within its own tempestuous logic, it made of this crucifixion the base of a new, unheard-of religion.

This was the gap between Jesus and his hearers. Once one has succeeded in breaking the thick hard crust of familiarity that surrounds his words, one has the impression that life, for Christ, was the thing itself: a continuously, tempestuously developing situation. Whereas for them it was a series of still tableaux, a series of situations, each one greeted with surprise. *That* is why, to jolt them out of the placid mentality in which man has listened to sermons since the world began, Christ reminds them of their own experience, of the cruelty of this world, of the law's delays, of the blatant triumph of moral wrong. To make his own special devastating point, he will go to any lengths. He is quite prepared to compare his own beloved Father to a lazy judge who will at last bestir himself to shake off an importunate widow. *Anything* to get the spark going across the gap that separates God from the real in the mind of man, an insulation so effective that man is not even conscious of it, and yet it becomes terribly evident in the complacency of religious people when with astounding naïveté they think to pass God's judgment on the prostitute.

The contrast between Christ's attitude to the people the gospel calls sinners and his attitude to the self-righteous whom it does not call sinners is well known. Of course he doesn't condone the ways of these 'sinners', but I think we are over-anxious to say this, being concerned to preserve intact our tidy moral universe and so restore the static religious world that Christ came to tear into. It is not in his contact with the 'sinners' that the *crisis* of the gospel appears. *There* he can show himself simply as the saviour, simply dissolving sin in his gracious approach. It is in the contact with official religion that the crisis appears whose only solution is the Cross. There the essential confrontation, there the struggle of man's godliness with God's humanity.

In reply to our impertinent question: 'What is Christ trying to do to his hearers?', I answer, presumptuously, that I think he is trying to get people to *live*. Christ is urging his followers to become completely alive to themselves in the tempestuous flux of earthly existence and *there* to abandon themselves to God, *there* to discern, impossibly, the lineaments of God's face. If we are afraid even to live, how shall we ever bear the beauty and terror and comfort of God?

This was an appeal that Christ alone could make. For only with the coming of Christ was this life of ours ripe to die into God. Only at that point in human history could life's claim on us be identified with God's claim. Christ was rushing – and how tempestuous the gospel is, how absurdly unlike the Religious Books of the world – towards the definitive and God-designed crisis of human growth; all his resources as a teacher are deployed towards jogging us on to this new path into human fulness which is fulness of God.

In this vitality of Christ, unique alike in its intensity and in the conviction of its bearer that here vitality is the sign of God's presence: in this vitality whose pressure on the hearers is the simple urgency of God himself, we sense already the pressure of the Resurrection, the new world. In the old world God's command was two-fold: live, and do my will. It was indeed almost: live, *but* do my will. In Christ, God's command becomes single. It is simply: live: let the life that you *are* come out. Faced with the dual command, man is problematic and agnostic. For the demands of life, seeming to conflict with God's claim or at least to lie outside its reach, represent a portion of reality that is without God. If this is so, God becomes limited and so non-existent. Only in Christ does God make upon man a single, simple, inclusive, and thus a self-authenticating claim. And in the words of Christ, taken in their full existential impact, this self-authenticating claim of God is felt.

And as it is impossible to think of this Christ-event as discontinuous with the preceding human story, it is necessary to see the life that spoke in Christ as a final and revelatory stage of human evolution.

Can we now understand more fully the most famous and lyrical passage in the gospels – the sermon on the birds of the

JESUS'S TEACHING · 77

air and the lilies of the field? When we really think about it, how unobvious this passage is, how wrongly we associate it with the beautiful truisms of which most religious literature is composed. For religious truisms are to be taken literally, and if we took this sermon literally we should starve and so incur God's wrath and, I think, Christ's laughter. Indeed we should be a perfect example of those 'children of light' whom Christ chidingly advises to take a leaf out of the book of the 'children of this world'.

It is not a piece of pious moralizing. It is a picture, trembling with life, of the way Christ is pointing. The gay lilies, unspoiled by thought, show to us in all their careless beauty the life that pulsates unconsciously in our veins. We *are* that life, we cannot escape it, we must live it and be it: and then we too shall be invested in its carefree splendour, hearing with every fibre of our being Christ's words: 'If God so clothes the lilies of the field, *that are today and tomorrow are cast into the oven . . .*'. There is the punch-line. *There* is the bewildering conflux of perspectives opened up by the gospel of Christ: the lilies of the field, sheer life, contrasted with the timorous pacings of religious man, and *then* brought to *death*. *We* must wear the gay smile of those flowers, so that all may come to associate Godliness with life and freedom, knowing that thus we are on the sure way to death and through death with our brave leader.

This precarious living, which is really the tragic and humorous situation of man filled with new meaning and pointed to an eternal destiny (rather than retreated from into 'religion'): this precarious living, which alone bears a worthy witness to the living God and frees him from the travesty that religion so easily makes of him, is wonderfully described by Paul:

Honour and dishonour, praise and blame, are alike our lot: we are the imposters who speak the truth, the unknown men whom all men know; dying we still live on; disciplined by suffering, we are not done to death; in our sorrows we have always cause for joy; poor ourselves, we bring wealth to many; penniless, we own the world. (2 Cor. 6: 6 ff.)

Is the time not at hand when the Church will once again show this image to the world?

7

God Again

WE CANNOT KNOW GOD-HIMSELF BY ANY EFFORT OF our understanding. The come-back, 'yes, but God can make himself known to us', also creates difficulties. For if God is to make himself known, this must be through our experience: and how then could we know that it was God who was showing himself in that experience?

The Christian doctrine answers this difficulty by refusing to talk in terms of 'God getting through to us'. The mysterious statement it makes instead is that God has embraced us in his own eternal self-expression. Integral to the Christian concept of revelation is the notion of an eternal self-expression of God. A self-expression of God that would be only 'to us' is impossible. It encounters the difficulty inherent in the 'God getting through' idea, and fails to surmount it.

Now the notion of 'God building us into his self-expression' is founded on the Incarnation, which is not, in the last analysis, a matter of God translating himself to us in human terms. It is primarily the creation of a new situation, in which God is saying to a parcel of flesh and blood what he says eternally to his Word: 'Thou art my Son, this day have I begotten thee.' And Christian man knows God, not as a parcel of flesh and blood believed to be a making-visible of the invisible, but by being himself built-into the parcel of flesh and blood that is God's eternal Word, that is 'in God'. This gives us the Christian God concept that we have been compelled impertinently to call new because there is so little attempt to formalize it on the part of the Christian mind.

Doubtless the reason for this reluctance is the fear of expressions that savour of pantheism. For when we try to make formal and explicit the God-concept implied in the above interpretation of the Incarnation, we find ourselves saying something like this: God is the situation in which Christ-enlightened man finds himself. He is the inclusive situation to which man awakes: the situation, of course, itself awakening man to itself and to himself in it. In static terms, this is saying that God is the whole of which we are parts. The Christian doctrine avoids pantheism, not by denying this proposition but by refusing from the outset the static type of thinking in which it arises.

By the Incarnation and its 'Spiritual' extension in a community, man is built into God's self-disclosure. Dynamically he *becomes* that self-disclosure, so that with every advance towards the dynamic unification in God which this becoming *is*, he knows God the more. And the *connection* between this progressive human wholeness and oneness and the invisible God who is known in it is unique, *sui generis*. That is to say, it is not the relation of effect to its cause, not a case of man's knowing the Creator 'by the things that are made', but a unique elucidation, illumination of man by the original meaning.

Thus the Christian understanding of God is wholly in terms of a human situation. This works in a manner which avoids the two pitfalls to which knowledge of God is prone. The pitfall of regarding God as an object known in itself is avoided by insisting that the terms we use are human terms and apply to man not God, *describe* man not God. The other pitfall, of regarding God as merely the presumed cause of certain effects, is avoided by the insistence that the human reality in question is not *outside* God but is situated by God's grace in God as the extension of his incarnate Word. Against the first mistake the Christian understanding insists on the non-divinity of the directly known, but against the second it insists on the divinity of the indirectly known. Though it is really averse to the distinction of direct and indirect knowledge.

The Christian understanding of God might seem to be adopting position A (knowledge of *man*) to oppose position B (knowledge of *God*), and then adopting position B to oppose position A. But in fact it refuses from the start the whole style of thinking for which these positions arise as exhaustive alternatives: 'We must know God either "in himself" or "through his effects".' To state the case thus is to think of 'God' and 'things' as objects, between which an order of cognition has to be found. This procedure is un-Christian.

The more we penetrate to the heart of the Christian understanding, the more we realize that the humanness of the known not only does not distract from the God so known but positively enhances the intimacy and directness of the knowledge of God. What is said *is said of man* – that he is gathered into one – and it is not straining human terms to embrace a divine object. And somehow the very fact that the human terms are not thus extended beyond the human allows what *is* beyond the human to show itself as the inclusive and embracing reality.

We are taught to think in this dynamic way by the Bible. The Bible is not content to say that God helps us, protects us, etc. It calls *God* 'our help', 'our shield', 'our stronghold' – substantives that tend to stick to the human reality whose divine betterment they describe. In the end, in the full unfolding, the substantive comes as it were finally to rest in the human and, conversely rather than paradoxically, God is then fully revealed. For God in the New Testament is 'our gathering into one', and 'our gathering into one' is 'us gathered', is 'the gathering', in the sense of 'a motley gathering': while he who 'is' our gathering is fully revealed as the enclosing All.

The Church knows God. The Church reveals God. But the punch-line is THAT THE CHURCH KNOWS GOD BY REVEALING HIM. She does not know God first and *then* pass on what she knows. Her style of knowing depends on, *is*, her bodying-forth of the eternal Word. The divine *elucidation* of man is logically prior to the divine *illumination* of him. The witness is of the community precisely *as* this community. It has seemed to me that the task today is to convert this knowing, which the Church has and is, into *understanding*.

A Note on Theologians

One learns theology in order to be able to talk of God to the people of our time. The addition 'of our time' is hardly necessary, the situation that makes it seem so being itself highly abnormal. Yet the study of theology is highly complex. And while the only justifying end-product is 'talk about God to contemporary man', the matter of this talk is not just personal reflection however wise, but historically revealed and historically developed truth. Hence the need for a method-ology, with all that that implies in the way of specialized historical knowledge, etc. Such prodigious toil exhausts our theologian! In reality he has only got to the beginning of 'being a theologian', but he *feels* he has got to the end. If his desire to be relevant has not become totally dormant, he will want to push out a few paperbacks. But he will see this task as no more than the effort, itself considerable, to put into contemporary or 'ordinary' language what he knows already in technical language. And this task is *quite* different from the task one imposes on oneself when, full of theological learning, one sits down and asks oneself 'What the hell does it all mean?', a question that is asked about *life* and not merely about the mass of learning accumulated.

It is only the attempt to answer *this* question, put wholly and honestly to oneself and with a preparedness to hear answers from unexpected quarters, that can issue in a real theology. Paradoxically, the shirking of this task is more of a danger today than ever before. For not only does the far greater amount of learning required exacerbate the factor of exhaustion. In addition to this, *within the privileged circle of professional theology* an original and adventurous mind will, through the modern theological disciplines, arrive at very radical shifts of perspective and involve the theologian in violent clashes with his conservative peers, so that he easily comes to think that by these shifts and in these consequent clashes he is being 'contemporary'. He will easily fail to realize that what is *within the circle* a revolution appears to the wider world (that is waiting to hear from him) to be a purely domestic battle, offering no more than the journalistic interest of a palace revolution.

Note on Niebuhr

I heard last night a moving lecture by Reinhold Niebuhr to American divinity students. His drift was: 'Our preaching is hopeless, because all we do is to tell people to be loving. But we all know we ought to be loving, and we also know that we can't and aren't. Hence the boring irrelevance, the "only too true" character of our preaching. Our preaching will continue to be platitudinous till we preach again of "grace".' That's fine. But he seemed to be offering a conception of grace simply as *enablement* for loving. There was no idea, so far as I could gather, of grace as the wholeness that comes to us in and through the *breakdown of loving* which, more radically, is the breakdown *in* loving, with all that involves in the way of tragic and comic human experience. Grace does not enable-to-work a system which, without it, does not work, the system being a constant in this transition. It breaks down the system. And, paradoxically, in so doing it brings us closer to 'nature', the nature that the system had to immobilize and bring under the control of will.

8

What about Natural Theology then?

IT WILL PROPERLY BE ASKED: IS THERE ANY PLACE in your system for what is called natural theology, the knowledge about God that is available to the rational enquiring mind? Are you not insinuating that there are only two positions possible: that of Christian belief and commitment, in which God is known through the believer's death and resurrection, and that of 'unregenerate man' for whom existence must be in the last resort without meaning?

Yes, I think that those are the alternatives. And superficially considered, they appear to leave no room for a natural theology. But when we come to spell out these alternatives, we see that this is not the case. Let us consider the man who is drawn towards the Christian faith 'because otherwise existence is meaningless'. Now two things are to be considered here: the appeal of the Christian faith, 'as giving meaning', and the *demand*, on the part of the man's experience itself, 'that it have meaning'. And now focus on the latter consideration. Here am I, a man of this time, taking stock of all that I know and am. Now suppose I come to the conclusion that there is no ultimate meaning in all this. The Church comes along and says 'I will give it all meaning'. Then I accept the Church. What, in that case, has happened? What exactly have I chosen? Not 'meaningfulness' but 'a release from meaninglessness', which is a vastly different thing. It is an *escape*, from a world without meaning, into, well what? An escape is a dead end.

The debate between the existentialist – one thinks especially of Camus – and the Christian so easily ends up with the Christian in the escapist position. The Christian agrees with Camus's statement of life, and *then* says 'but this is intolerable, *therefore* I embrace the faith'. The irony is that the Christian 'went into existentialism' intending to clear Christianity of the charge of escapism. In fact, the type of Christian thinking that emerges in this context has a perceptibly escapist quality. It tends also to be selective in its human interests, ignoring the world of modern science. It is an 'Arts' Christianity. It really took a false step at the beginning in accepting the existentialists' world-picture, which is in reality a 'private view', reflecting the special preoccupation of some intellectuals. Existentialism as a philosophy does not succeed in breaking into the world of our time. It is fastidiously withdrawn from the common insight that is today coming to birth. It belongs to the old world – not indeed of the armchair philosopher but still of the 'intellectual'. The novels of James Baldwin give one just as stark a picture as those of Sartre and Camus, but they *breathe* in a way the latter do not. The supernatural is savagely *denied*, but is it not *methodically* excluded, giving the feeling that the existentialists' 'bleak world' is contrived.

In short, it may well be that Christian faith alone gives the meaning. But the *demand for meaning* must be inscribed in this world of ours. Otherwise it cannot be meaning, but only an escape that the Christian faith offers.

Let us see, then, if we can deploy an *argument* for belief in God.

Argument

Movement has always puzzled the philosopher. But the nature of the puzzle is different today from what it was for Aristotle. Aristotle asked *why* anything moved. Today we ask what movement *means*: 'Is there any sense in it?' Aristotle's answer, briefly, would have been no. Movement as such was not intelligible. A moving body was neither here nor there. A growing youth, precisely *as* growing, was neither boy nor man. The mind could latch on to the point of departure and to the point of arrival. But the actual *process* curiously evaded the mind. But was Aristotle curious about the evasion? I don't think so. He regarded movement as being beneath the mind's grasp, rather than beyond it (as Bergson seems to have thought). Process, like matter, was a kind of surd.

I mentioned the growing youth as an example of movement. For Aristotle, the growth of a boy *was* movement, just as much as the passage of a billiard ball. *And it was equally unintelligible.* And here we come to another big difference between Aristotle and ourselves. For not only are we fascinated by the simplest movement, as Aristotle wasn't, but we are *more* fascinated by the more complex processes, as Aristotle wasn't. Here I probably do him an injustice, for Aristotle was a keen observer in the field of biology. Still, he would, I think, have insisted that if you draw a circle round biological process *as process*, your circle would be enclosing something as simply baffling as the movement of a billiard ball. And, to insist, baffling as opposed to challenging.

Aristotle's interest was in the state the thing had arrived at after the move, and his answer to the question 'why does it move?' was, that something else that already had that state, had given it to the thing moved. A thing *gets* hot because it is in contact with something that *is* hot.

With Newton's laws of motion, a totally new thought-process appears. For an intelligible pattern is found in movement itself. This is a tremendous liberation for the mind, and a transformation of the universe. World process, hitherto regarded as casual and unintelligible, revealed itself – at least in this simple matter of local motion – as a thing of order and beauty, a perfect partner to mathematics.

Is 'to grasp the laws of motion' the same thing as 'to understand movement'? The only answer I can give to this difficult question is a mixture of 'no' and the question 'what would it mean, please, to understand movement?' I think, moreover, that the type of mind that best grasps the laws and their significance would be impatient with this question. It would want to say 'I perform, with regard to local movement, the requisite act of understanding, and that's all there is to it. If by "understand" you mean some sort of obscure penetration into the essence of movement, then I'm not interested.' And this confessed limitation of interest is wholly characteristic of the modern scientific mind. It has been well observed by Laurence Bright, O.P., that whereas the classical philosopher asked what was the *essence* of something, the modern thinker asks 'What's happening? What's going on here?' And of course for the classical mind there *was* no essence of movement. There were only essences of *things*, exact definitions of which were sought. Thus the classical mind was *more* ambitious about *fewer* realities, whereas the modern mind is *less* ambitious, but turns its modest scrutiny to *all* realities.

Now within the limits of this new, methodical direction of intelligence to the understanding of movement, a rather exciting thing was to happen. It was sparked off by a further discovery: of the structure of the atom and of the structure of the living cell, *and of a certain affinity between them*. More precisely, it is the molecule that bears this resemblance. Both could be regarded as systems-in-movement, to be systematically understood – understood, that is, as the laws of motion are understood, in terms of 'how it works'.

Now, of this affinity, two interpretations are possible. We might say that the living cell is merely a more elaborate version of the molecule, and so build up a *mechanical* understanding of the universe. But we might equally say that the molecule is a less interesting version of the cell. And we might add that the cell is not only more interesting in the sense of more complex. For we might say that this increase in complexity carries with it *another factor*, which is difficult to name but seems to be forcing itself on our attention as the real thing to focus on. The point is that with the consideration of the cell, 'system-in-movement' is beginning to make sense. It is as though the world, first considered as systems-in-movement and calling forth from the mind merely an admiration of order and tidiness, were now beginning to *reveal* itself to us. And whereas we would say of the atomic and molecular structures that we 'understood' them merely in the way that, with the aid of Newton's laws, we 'understand' movement, we are inclined to say of the *living* structure that we really do *understand* it, that we feel a certain affinity between it and our mind, that we find it congenial, rather as we understand people, that is to say by empathy or what the schoolmen called connaturality. And we might find ourselves saying that our own consciousness had something to do with this understanding, our consciousness that emphatically asserts the simplest systems to be as it were run-down versions of the more complex, rather than the other way round.

A generalized theory of evolution excitingly confirms this hunch. And this not merely by its contention that the simplest systems *have* coalesced into the more complex – for this after all would only be telling us how the universe was built up. We should still not be accounting for the exciting sense that the universe was progressively *revealing* itself to us. The theory of evolution only elucidates *this* notion when we consider that *consciousness itself is the term of this development*.

Of course the living cell is more meaningful than the molecule, *because it is closer to ourselves*. Thus we get a picture of the universe as *converging on consciousness* and becoming meaningful in itself as the things we study get more like ourselves.

It is rather difficult to describe this crucial stage in the argument without traducing the central insight. We traduce the insight if we imply a picture of man looking at the universe and seeing in it a system of mirrors becoming increasingly polished and self-reflecting. The point is that the structures, as they converge on ourselves, become, absolutely, more intelligible. It is not that we think they are more intelligible, whereas in *reality* they are only more like us. Were this the case, we should not have a mounting excitement, but a decreasing excitement, or rather a mounting excitement that turned out to be unjustified. The fact that the structures become more like ourselves does not *answer* the question of meaning that they raise. It voices the question with unprecedented vigour. 'We' don't answer the question. We *are* it. The universe converges on us, but it does not close in on ourselves. It opens out in us.

A further point can be made here. We may have started the enquiry into the universe as spectators. But the enquiry converges on the consciousness that is its spur, and consciousness is indivisible and means *me* in the whole dynamic of my existence, means me *who must act*, means me who am involved and precisely *not* a spectator. And retrospectively, the very first and simplest insights into structures are realized to have implied involvement as against simple looking-on.

Further, as the living cell is not really reducible to the simpler systems, and breaks down into them only at the cost of its own life, so the supreme product, consciousness, is irreducible. The law of understanding the less complex in the light of the more complex, and not vice versa, is supremely verified in the consciousness on which the whole universe converges. *Consciousness in* which and *to* which the universe reveals its meaning.

And with the whole universe thus seen to converge on consciousness, the God-question is put up, not merely because a sense of humour forbids us to say that we are the ultimate meaning of all we survey, but because of a radical incompleteness in the understanding afforded by the notion of convergence-on-consciousness. This convergence is not so much the point of arrival as a point of no return. We are committed now to a final adventure in consciousness, involving us together, of which the conduct is not in our hands. This commitment was slowly and unknowingly building up as the excitement of a self-revealing universe mounted.

How much *can* we say at this point? Can we for instance say that consciousness is not only irreducible to its elements but, unlike the successive life-forms that build up to it, unable to be conceived of as itself dying into something higher? I think we can. For when we come to persons, coalescence ceases to be their total absorption but is on the contrary their personal enrichment. At the same time it is rather fascinating to note that the Christian Revelation comes as close to the notion of a 'death of persons into something higher' as is possible without overriding the new rule of coalescence-without-absorption, the rule of love. It posits a new love that is, while remaining love, in the order of mutation, a love whose source and norm is death-resurrection.

How all this should flower into a natural theology is not altogether clear. But I feel that this unclarity is due to *embarras de richesse*. For we seem to have, conjoined, the two classical approaches to God from the purely human starting-point, associated respectively with Augustine and Aquinas. Aquinas started with 'the world', Augustine with the human heart. 'Thou hast made us for thyself, and our heart is restless till it rests in thee.' In my line of argument the whole world (what interested Aquinas) becomes restlessness in man (what interested Augustine) and, in man, seeks the meaning. Man is the insomnia, the fever of the universe. In him, the *restlessness* of the universe becomes a *questioning*.

If I have failed adequately to map out man's quest for God in the form of an argument, what has become clear is the nature of that quest, its situation in man's conscious life, or rather man's situation in *it*. Namely that God is the lodestar of *consciousness itself*, consciousness as such, rather than an object *within* consciousness. God does not properly figure in the inventory which man takes when he reviews his position in the world and among his fellows. For this inventory is already a 'sitting-back' from the nisus of conscious restless being. The above ramblings may be thus condensed:

Consciousness is movement becoming meaningful.
Conversely, in its light movement itself demands meaning.
In its light, and with itself as paradigm,
We pronounce life to be more intelligible than simple local movement, and intelligence more intelligible than life.

At the same time, a most profound exigence of consciousness is satisfied by the notion that life is an evolved and sophisticated form of movement and consciousness itself an evolved and sophisticated form of life.

Finally, faced with the implication of all this, that consciousness centres the universe,
We find ourselves unable to think of ourselves as the centre and ground of all,
And so inevitably put up the God-question and suggest that all is ultimately grounded in an infinite and self-sufficing act of consciousness that is totally meaningful to itself.

Of this latter, all that we can say only emphasizes its incomprehensibility, as for instance the statement that here the

WHAT ABOUT NATURAL THEOLOGY THEN? · 93

distinction of subject and object loses all meaning. The finitude of consciousness shows itself precisely in the distinction of subject and object. Normally, subject and object communicate in the mystery of being: which mystery, imperfectly elucidated, holds subject and object in a distinction that is not a simple confrontation (which would make knowledge impossible). But where the idea of being is perfectly elucidated and thus escapes our grasp, the distinction of subject and object also disappears. 'The idea of being, perfectly elucidated' equates with 'infinite consciousness', which is what wise men call God.

Note. Can we perhaps relate all this to the Christian understanding of God in the following way? The ascent of the mind to God is based on our understanding of our continuity with the whole universe. But unregenerate man (man half-alive and half-dead, as opposed to man wholly dead and wholly alive) can appreciate this continuity only with his intellect. It is only in the saving dissolution that he becomes fully at one with all and so fully responsive to the All.

First, then, it is myth-making to start with God. For the only *real* line on God that we can have is through an intense experience of this world and of our involvement in it. God is the light at the other end of this dark night. But the God who is thought of as first of all on his own and then turning to the work of creating, is a God placidly conceived apart from this agon. A God well within the limits of man's imagination – and the world he creates is 'reduced to scale'. It is only in a sort of dream-consciousness that this story gives meaning to man. When I cry out to God out of my human and cosmic depths, it is no solace to be told what 'God' (that sedate figure on the throne) has done for 'man' (that diminutive puppet who walks across God's stage).

Second. The Bible, assuredly, starts with 'In the beginning God created the heavens and the earth'. But the treatment that scholars give to these opening chapters reflects, by its complete difference from the treatment appropriate to the Exodus, the different position accorded to these chapters even by the uncritical Hebrew mind. They are not, unlike the Exodus, the documentation of the Jews' experience of God and – inextricably intertwined in this – of themselves as the People of God. They embody, rather, the Jewish 'monotheizing' revision of contemporary Babylonian myths. And this revision is dependent on that knowledge of the one God whose primary documentation is the growing self-awareness of the People of God. We are coming to realize what a fatal falsification of perspectives results from a catechetics that starts with the Fall of Man and rushes through the history of Israel to arrive at the divine remedying of that Fall in the New Testament.

Third. The Bible undoubtedly presents a fundamentally evolutionary vision. The living God has inserted himself in human experience as the future of a people. It is through this category that he has entered into the real live primary consciousness of man, as opposed to the dream-consciousness in which man escapes from the harsh realities of temporal existence into a timeless picture-world. But there is, necessarily, a limit to the extent to which the Jewish people could realize the implications of this divine insertion. This limit is twofold – in extent and in intensity. In regard to extent, the Jews necessarily regarded sacred history as their history. Only in occasional prophetic flashes was there a hint that it is the whole human race that is being driven on to the final fulfilment and that the new Jerusalem will be, essentially and on pain of not being itself, the home of all the nations. And with regard to intensity, the expected and striven-for term of the people's development was only transcendent in the negative sense that they were unable to rest at any stage, and, by implication, at *any imaginable* stage. The arrival at the final stage in Christ's resurrection lay beyond the scope of the people's expectation and in fact was expedited only through the peoples' rejection of Christ. St Paul does not say that the Jews *had* to reject Christ for Christ to become what he was meant to become, but he does insist that this connection between rejection and perfection is in the order of mystery, of that specifically divine conduct of the affairs of man that might be called a transfigured fatality.

But if the biblical cadre was hardly apt to take a sacred history that was universal in its scope and transcendent in its term, the Christ-event was both these things. And in the writings of Paul we see the biblical category of sacred history stretched to breaking-point in conveying this tremendous event.

Now the expression of this event does not, absolutely, require a new concept (of evolution on a universal scale and moving to a transcendent term). For the original expression is the event itself and the new community whose coming-to-be is the fulness of the event. The disciples were led beyond the confines of this world in the death and resurrection of Christ. And this was the crowning of a religious vision in which the divine was conveyed in and through a *developmental* view of life. The God who spoke to Moses was a God who was future, was to come, was the goal of the history on which Moses, in obedience to God, embarked. In the risen Christ, St Paul saw man arrived at that goal, arrived at God, and said as much.

Fourth. The universal and transcendent consummation of man, realized in the Christ, certainly seeks an evolutionary concept if man is going to receive it fully into his thought and life and culture. And this it has not yet found. The concept of 'sacred history' has something rather sedate about it. The reality that first appeared in the unique phenomenon of Israel and grew there till it burst into the Christ-explosion,

D

cooled into the static forms of the Greco-Roman world. It there became a story that started with God.

A thing that has struck me recently in Catholic discussion groups is that the type of problem raised tends to be remote from life – and what on earth *is* a *religious problem* that is remote from *life*? Something in our religious upbringing produces problems created by 'religion' in a void, a sort of dogmatic acrostic. Thus for instance 'the problem of original sin' is not a challenge to think in terms of a communal religious failure, and thus to look for a communal redemption, or to realize that sin and redemption are known respectively by the type of society that each results in. It is simply the problem as to why one sin of our first parents should be propagated with the propagation of the race. Our Christian story has started with God, who then *has* to be thought of as a blown-up human being: and his behaviour, in making one man and one woman and then visiting on an indefinitely multitudinous progeny the results of their disastrous mistake, is highly questionable. When her child comes home from school with 'O mummy, if only Adam and Eve hadn't eaten that apple!', a sensible woman must wonder whether the child is being taught any religion.

The nearest we get to reality in our religious problematizing is in the 'problem of evil'. But here too, our habit of starting with God causes the problem to be wrongly posed. Why did God make people like Hitler, hopelessly and helplessly deformed children, and a world prone to natural disaster on a prodigious scale? Of course the problem of evil will remain with us until the end of time, but it is *not* the problem of justifying such an impossible being. It is the problem of seeing any meaning in a twisted and tortured existence. And when the victim triumphs over his circumstances and affirms, against all the appearances, the goodness of life, we say '*there* is God'. The classic instance of this is the Tolstoy hero who, on the impossibly miserable retreat from Moscow, when he is only able to keep going by counting his steps up to a thousand and then beginning afresh, is suddenly given to affirm that just to exist is wonderful. 'Nothing almost sees miracles but misery.'

I was saying this the other night to a young man who had posed the problem of evil in conventional Catholic terms. At last he said, 'I see now that I've been leaning on God, leaning back on God, and that this is all wrong. God is in the future.' This subsequently suggested to me a couplet that more or less sums up what I have to say:

> The God on whom we lean is of our world,
> And with his death we too are lost in death.

('Of our world' means, of course, 'projected by us as a fixed point within our mental universe'.)

But is an evolutionary concept of God possible? If we mean 'God conceived of as the term of an evolutionary process', clearly not, for such a God would lack transcendence. But if we mean 'God as the meaning of the evolutionary concept', this is a more promising line.

For the concept of evolution is a tantalizing one. It seems to give meaning to the whole universe and yet, in the very act of giving meaning, raises the question of *its own* meaning. Something rather similar underlies the traditional argument to God 'from causality'. One thing was seen to be caused by another, then everything was said to be caused by some other thing: *then* we started wondering what 'cause' really meant. In the very act of making sense of things, it wanted to make sense itself, and thus insinuated the concept of a transcendent cause.

But the process of 'giving and demanding meaning' is much richer in the case of evolution than in the case of causality. Evolution makes incomparably more sense of this world than does causality, for it enables us to apprehend this world in its own dynamic reality, its dramatic *déroulement*. And correspondingly, it demands meaning far more urgently than does causality. Who has not been brought up all standing with the thought 'Where on earth is it all going?' This question, as it immediately and naïvely occurs, is the God-question. It could never have arisen in the world as Aquinas knew it, and this should jolt us into a greater awareness than we usually have of the difference between our two worlds, and of the immeasurably greater eloquence of our present science-explored world. The concept of evolution gives a quite new edge to the question 'What are we doing here?' which is normally paraphrased as the conventional religious question: 'Who put us here, and for what purpose?' Conventionally understood, the question is answered with a God who then proceeds to be 'the beginning of the story'. With the evolutionary edge on it, the question emphatically is *not* answered with such a God. It demands meaning, not information.

There is another reason why the concept of evolution is so potent theologically. Evolution makes sense because it converges on consciousness. The concept of evolution tantalizes us with the force of consciousness itself. Thus it impels consciousness to seek its own meaning. And this means *us* in the whole of our living, moving, projecting reality.

The Christian tradition has shied away from those movements of thought – pre-eminently Marxism – that have sought the meaning of the present in a Utopian future to which it is supposed to be tending. The reaction is understandable, for such movements seem to deny the irreducible significance of each personal life as it unfolds, which is of crucial moment for the Christian. But the reaction is as superficial as is the understanding of evolution that has provoked it. For this understanding has confined itself to the *term* of evolution and seen the evolutionary process as significant only as producing that term. This way of thinking is the antithesis of the evolutionary concept, which is precisely the expression of that new-found intelligibility in process which has inspired the momentous scientific developments of the last four hundred years.

Once we see evolution as the challenge and enrichment of the scientific spirit, realizing that for the scientist the question 'What is going on?' is the vital question: and then discover that evolution thus considered demands meaning as potently as it gives it; then we discern a profound affinity between evolutionary thinking and the Christian interest in 'now'. The concept of evolution illuminates the Christian 'now', because the latter is full of awareness of transience and contingency, of the *responsio mortis* that is in every moment of Christian time. The God in whose name Christians have turned away from an evolving world is 'the God on whom we lean', not the God who transfigures each moment in dissolution. The God who was the meaning of Israel, who exploded in the Christ-event as universalized meaning, may at last, in this evolutionary age, be thought of as the meaning of the universalized meaning-giving and meaning-demanding concept of evolution.

Note. The treatment of the Greco-Roman influence has been farouche and over-simplified, implying that this precipitation of the Christian vision in the forms of the Greco-Roman world need not and should not have happened. But this would be to say in effect that the Church should not have spread over the world, that this particular fusion of the Hebraic and the classical should not have taken place. Which would be a denial of all that the Church stands for.

In point of fact, the evolutionary mentality that is ours simply did not exist in the ancient world. So there was nothing in the converted world that *needed* to exploit the evolutionary meaning of the Christian Thing. That world brought its own pagan culture to the font, where it was transformed to the maximum extent compatible with remaining itself, the requisite vehicle of self-recognition for the men of that time. It is worth noting how the early converts brought with them whole chunks of doubtful mysticism and worse, which the Church took on and slowly changed. It is *today*, and not in its proper time, that the Greco-Roman version of the Christian Thing is a serious drug on the religious market.

9

Recognition

TO CONSIDER THE HUMAN PERSON IN A REAL WAY is to encounter a paradoxical co-presence of wealth and poverty. He is at once somebody and nobody.

Specifically, a man is only 'somebody' pending his *recognition* by others. At every stage of his development we find him seeking this recognition, almost as the condition for his existence. Certainly recognition and acceptance is the condition *in* which we exist and flourish, even if the philosopher must judge it sheer contradiction to suggest that this recognition alone brings us into being. As a proposition this *is* absurd, yet it might be allowed not as a strict proposition but as a dramatic comment on the absurdity that is built into the human condition. A man is a question addressed to his fellows. Without their answer he does sheerly exist, but sheerly and merely to exist is intolerable to us. It can be done in the brave words of a somewhat pretentious philosophy. It cannot be done in fact.

We might tend to think that family and social life provide an adequate solution to this problem. But however successful the social solution it seems that there is a further dimension in which a recognition-problem arises. In the end, no-one can really tell me who I am. There are moments when I am painfully conscious that it is only by a sort of conspiracy that we reassure each other of each other's reality and worth. And the more discerning teenage rebel hears the hollow note in our exhortations to become a responsible member of society. Even if he gets beyond the suspicion that we thus exhort him only so that he shall not be a nuisance to us, he must still be aware that we wobble incoherently between an appeal to enlightened self-interest and an appeal to real generosity. He is asking who he is, in a tone of voice and with an urgency that precludes any and every answer we can give him. At this stage the parting of the ways between the Christian and the humanist will begin to appear, as the Christian prepares to *push* the evidence towards an ultimate identity crisis, while the humanist begins to *play down* the evidence. Neither is quite honest.

As I am not writing as an apologist, I must ask leave to suppose that the evidence does warrant the belief in an 'ultimate identity crisis'. For I'm not trying to prove my faith, but to understand it,

So I *am* asking 'who I am' in such a way that no one can tell me.

We have seen that ancient man got his answer to this question from 'the world'. He tamed the world and 'trained' it to give the answer, to accept him as a member of the cosmic household. The answer to the ultimate identity-question has of its nature to come from 'not-man', and the function of 'not-man' was supplied by a sacralized 'world'. This is a mythical solution, and the myth has been exploded. For the world was really giving an answer even less convincing than the answer of society. It was a more portentous answer, but a fictitious one. The world cannot talk. Or as the Japanese proverb has it, 'the wind cannot read'. Genesis gives us an inkling of this great truth, in the failure of Adam to find a mate in the animal kingdom.

We fail to obtain recognition from the world. But we can't then rise 'above' the world and seek it from 'God'. And this for a reason that at first appears to be simply human: that 'above the world' we are no longer *ourselves*, therefore no longer able to put the question: the question put by earthly man dies on the lips of 'metaphysical' man, who loses *himself* in speculation. But the pace quickens, the heart beats faster, when we realize that the real reason for the hopelessness of a 'metaphysical' answer is – of God. Inexorably we move towards a God who realizes us in our world. Inexorably because it is with our world, it is with the world in us, that we *move*, and, with all that we have and are and have not and are not, we batter on the doors of . . .

If only one could formulate the big question in its own native terms! In it, man seeks recognition from . . . We want new words here, for man presenting himself to the stars. We seek a recognition-of-us for which our difficulty in finding the right words is already an exploration into God, having about it that curious quality of being-led yet not knowing exactly how to put it.

This thing which we are seeking *is to do with the human person*. It is the ultimate personal justification of man. It is the concept for the God who comes, who saves, who justifies. In the rather special philosophical terms with which we seek to be philosophic in the Christian encounter context, the Christian Event is 'the coming of the personal in our world'. It is the revelation of the personal in a situation that does not succeed of itself in being personal, although composed of persons. To the question 'is the "person" of this revelation man or God?' we are entitled by our self-imposed limits to decline an answer. And in support of this reticence we may recall that the existential and dynamic language of the Bible identifies God with his coming and even with what he confers on man – for even the systematic theologian is constrained to accord to the uncreated grace (which strictly *is* God) the attribute of quasi-formal cause, and one robust patristic formula has it that regenerate man is composed of 'body, soul, and Holy Spirit'. God clothes man with himself. The Christian understanding of God is the understanding of this clothing of man, and the symbolism of clothing is the symbolism appropriate to the whole identity question.

The sign and sacrament of this clothing is a new relation of man to his world. In this relation, man is clothed trans-ceremoniously with this world – not with insignia taken *from* this world and cut to the cultured stones of a crown, but with the world as man natively meets it, lives it, and does in it. The New Man is decked out by God, for the divine encounter, in his own blood, not ritually but brutally and historically shed. And it is in his basic relationship to this world – in eating, in mating, in living and dying – that Christian man enters sacramentally into the encounter where he is eternally recognized.

10

A Meditation, a Query, and a Celebration

Meditation

The notion of my death being simply future is self-contra-
dicting
for it implies that when the time comes will be the time to
accept it
and this implies that *then* I shall be ready for it
whereas I know in the very fibre of my being, my self,
that I can never be ready, adequate for death.
The person, then, who will be ready when the time comes is
another person
and the death I look upon as simply future is someone else
dying
so that what I *call* my death is really someone else's death
and this is the self-contradiction in which most of us, most of
the time, pretend to live.
Indeed it is but a pretended life for there is no God in it.
For if my death is not present to me then neither is God
present.

If I am not now as one dead, there is no God.
For it is only with the whole of my existence that I can
reach out to God,
we can only reach out to God with the actual inbuilt movement of our being,
and this movement *is* movement, a pressure on the future,
the future present to the spirit.
What most people call the future is simply a totally different
set of circumstances around another self,
and this is not the future, but simply another situation.
It is in such another situation that most people locate their death:
and, their death meaninglessly future, they invoke a God who
is therefore meaninglessly present.
He alone is single whose death is present dissolution, exposure
to God.
He alone is single who presses forward with the whole of
himself into the unknown that is God.
All agree in associating death with God,
only to the unreflective God is on the other side of death,
on the other side of this meaningless future event – and now:
associated, then, with a future self that does not exist and
a present self that is not really alive.
In reality, God is the meaning of death being at once present
and future.
The thought of death dissolves our temporal perspective
and God is the meaning of this dissolution.
We cannot anticipate death, nor can we postpone it: we can
only live it
and this is to live God.
If we did not know we were going to die,
we could not call on God,
and this certainly not because there would then be no thought
of an after-life, but because there would then be, now, no
life that could meaningfully stretch out to God.

It is only by our death that the Invisible Light can cast a
shadow over our time,
For death is impossible whichever way you take it, however
you juggle with it, and God the incomprehensible is only
apprehended in the impossible.
The impossible in man, that is the restless striving that nothing
can satisfy.
But why is death the condition of God being real?
Because death is the inbuilt questioning of the ego which, if it
ignores this questioning, can have no God but one of its
own invention.
For death, my death, is the denial of my cherished illusion:
that I am separate, that I am not of any world, that I am
a world to myself.
There is no sense in such a being, and so there is no God for
it.
Such a being is precisely the fool who says in his heart: there
is no God.

Query

What you have offered, it will be urged, is a philosophy, a way
of life, a tao,
and not the Revelation of God.
What you have described is man confronting death and
raising the God-question
and not the son of God dying to raise a fallen world.
Your central figure is Rodin's Penseur, naked, posed, posing
the question.
Not the Christ seated on a stone, recovering what there was
to recover of breath and life after the scourging.
Worse, is it not a human gnosis posing as the Christian faith,
insufferably pretentious?
No, what I have described are the elements of an act that only
God could set in motion,

the stage-props of an act that only God could put on.

For consider man as I have pictured him, confronted with
impossible death, in search of meaning:

Consider him well: meaningless to himself as he thinks of
himself in his capsule of self apart from death, apart from
the turning world:

What can he do, what would I have him do?

Who can live man as I have placed him, drama of the world in
which he is lost?

What conceivable *event* is there that would be his passage
through death

into the whole, the meaning, the world community, God?

Clearly there is no such event conceivable in the terms of a
philosophy of life,

there is only the philosophy itself, dramatized,

only the infinity of human posturings before the Riddle of Life,

an infinite number of variations on a common theme,

provided by every literature, every sarcophagus with its
piece of undistinguished verse,

but no Event: the Event is of God, Advent of God.

What I have given is only the human structure of a divine
event,

divine event in man, advent in man.

The structure of the God-question in man is, reversed, the
answer of God.

Only God can put this show on.

And this leads me to wonder whether, as I confront my death
and wonder and wonder,

I am not really a kind of impostor,

considering an event that I shall certainly undergo, but whose
proper and adequate subject is one who holds the whole
world in his grasp.

For consider: I do see my death as the end of the world, I do
find inscribed in my mortal flesh an Apocalypse.

And so, as I approach death, am I not approaching an act
    which demands of the actor that he be world-represent-
    ative?
Is not death a liturgy in search of a priest?
And has not Christ, in appropriating death, achieved the
                    appropriate in place of the huge anomaly
which makes of man the fantastic question-mark that he is?
For Godless Christless man confronting death wrestles in his
    mind with an impossible conjunction of the tragic and
    the trivial, the grandiose and the absurd, the significant
    and the casual.
The sign of this anomaly is the Great Pyramid: so big that it
    crushes the mind and makes the heart beat in a panic void
housing two little parcels of dust
joined once by the royal rites of love.

Celebration

It will be great, it will be wonderful,
it will be heaven when we give up together the solitary
                                                    struggle
that has divided us for longer than anyone can remember,
that has worn us down to smooth pebbles
clicking together, the language of ordinary communication
filling the time and getting nowhere.
He who has but glimpsed this brotherhood that awaits us,
    that waits on us, who has just felt it trying to dissolve
    the struggle,
knows heaven and hell in a single sweetness of being.
For the present there is no release, save in moments of sin,
which are only moments of sin because they are only
                                                    moments:
For the brotherhood is entered either whole and entire and for
                    life, or it is not entered at all.

And it is thus entered only in faith, and the discreet and gentle
    love that goes with faith, and the hope that smiles on
    despair.
In faith, yes, but remember
that with every act of love God comes afresh,
and that to say that he comes in faith alone
is not to deny, as many would have it deny,
that the meeting of two or three in a real event of mutual
               discovery,
and the larger mutations of man in society
are the primary language of God's coming among us
and that in the constant surprise of mutual understanding
the community really does explore further into the depths of
               God.
This we must believe, if we believe, with all the 'progressive'
               theologians,
that the community itself is the sacrament of divine encounter.
Those who deny this do so, they think, from fear of illumin-
               ism,
from fear of perverting the faith into a gnosis.
But what they are really afraid of is love, truth torn out of its
               conceptual swaddling bands.
What they think is a fear for faith is really a fear of love.
We cannot go on for ever perfecting a progressive theology
and putting off the beginning.
And it is important to know that sin
snatches its trophies from that greater world,
and that conversion discovers to the sinner the beauty in sin,
               and so is shocking to everyone but God.

Lament

It is a terrible sadness, it is the sickness in us,
that we live, and carry on all the necessary commerce of
    living, and enter with brash cheerfulness into all the

delicate relationships that life imposes and means to be
    real life,
that we do all this and are all this
in terrible ignorance of the direction
taken for us by our whole existence.
Not only are we ignorant – in which there is some dignity,
but we render our very ignorance trivial, unimportant, totally
                uninhibiting of our working of the machine
which thus becomes in real fact a machine
coining the appropriate comment
consigning our dead to God knows what limbo between
                human concern and the terror of God.
Of course we would never be casual with 'God',
we would never make bad thoughtless half-meant jokes about
                                                'him':
But we do just this, we are just this way with that in our
                lives which really *is* God.

11

Eternal Life (1)

THE GOSPEL MESSAGE IS NOT ABOUT ANOTHER KIND of life, called *'eternal* life'. It is the statement that in Christ life is eternal.

Biblical films are always ghastly, but they always give me an image or two. Here is one such, from *The Greatest Story Ever Told*:

Christ preaching in the hot sun, to people hardened by weather and poverty and inured to brutality. Scarred, weather-beaten, life-moulded faces. Eternal life. He offers eternal life. He announces a passionate simplification. Love your brother and you have eternal life.

But was it all so simple? What precisely was the commitment that Christ required: a commitment to him personally, or a commitment to his teaching? 'Both' is no answer, though it is the usual one even today, when genuine truth-seeking persons see this problem as *the* difficulty with orthodox Christianity. The church seems to be demanding, *as well as* 'living for others', a specific religious confession which, if it has to be *distinguished from or added to* 'life for others', hardly deserves the name of commitment.

To avoid the equivocations into which people who talk about 'life' easily slip, we must first analyse the concept of life. The main distinction is between 'life', meaning the complex phenomenon in which we are involved and of which we do not have ultimate control, and the life that we recommend people to *lead*. Between the 'life' we tell people they have to accept, and the life we commend to them as a good life.

From this distinction there follows another, between religion and morality. Religion means what we do about the life we can't control. We can't do anything about this kind of life, but finding this ignorance and powerlessness unbearable we call in God to jolly us along. Whereas morality means what we do about the life we *can* control.

Now if we invoke a special sort of morality, namely a morality of love, the distinction between 'life lived' and 'life led' becomes less clear-cut, at least once we recognize that 'love your neighbour' as a pure categorical imperative will not do. For once we see that we can't love through clenched teeth – for by the time the decision has been taken, our neighbour is no longer there except as the object of our patronage – we realize that love involves a certain surrender to life in its basic, non-controlled, untidy wholeness.

Yet the relation between love and the 'life' to which it is the surrender is problematic. How far should we surrender to life? This in itself is a peculiar question. Can there be a 'limited surrender'? Presumably not. And yet a complete surrender, a complete going-with, seems to turn love into anarchy. And so it would seem to be impossible either to describe, or to implement, love in terms of surrender-to-life. 'Life' seems doomed to play an equivocal role: rightly accusing the prudent of not loving, and yet engulfing the generous in its own anarchic drives.

So with a morality of love, life-as-a-whole and life-as-lived start wanting to get together. Correspondingly, religion and morality start wanting to unite – and this is not merely in the sense of morality fulfilling the command of religion. But they can't get together. The position is complicated.

For Christ, the position is not complicated at all. That is the point of Christ. That is the message of Christ.

Christ takes the elements of this problem and fuses them together in the fire of a personal simplicity. Life as he sees it is (*a*) totally itself, a whole developing situation (*b*) totally livable in love. If you ask him, 'Where, in this business of surrender, do you draw the line?' he will answer 'I don't.' And if you insist: 'But you do, you must. You don't surrender to every impulse,' he will answer 'I only stop where life itself stops. My message is: the lilies of the field growing to their death, and the love of the brethren. And this is only *one* message. Yes, I know, the first is a statement of fact, the second is what I suppose you would call an injunction, but can't you SEE?'

What can't we see? What is this consuming and unanswerable impatience that stepped into our world and transformed it?

Christ is Revelation. Christ proclaims an identity between what we call life and what we call morality. To talk to Christ about morality would seem absurdly humourless. Christ proclaims an absolute significance in *life*, to be grasped in *love*. What we *called* religion and what we *called* morality become interchangeable in 'a self-evidently significant life for others'.

But we want to say to him, 'That's all very well. *You* see it that way. We don't. It isn't that way except in your vision.'

Christ replies: 'It *is* that way. It's not just the way I see it. What I see is the truth.'

We reply: 'Truth is a proposition.'

Christ: 'It is not. It is what I see and tell you. It is what I am.

The flowers of the field, the birds of the air, the love of the brethren. If you want facts, these are the facts. There is nothing else.'

We pause. We are not completely dim. We recognize that the disparate elements in us, the dues we pay to 'God' because 'life' is 'a mystery', and the love we give to the brethren, *head towards* an equation: that we cannot make the equation: but that we cannot answer Christ who does make it. For when he faces us with the love of our neighbour as the whole universe become single and articulate and banging on our doors, we know he's right. We know that his world, his world a single flame, is *the* world: the world as it lies under the gaze of God.

And yet if *we* cannot make the equation between 'life' and 'the way to live', it *must* be the case that the equation 'is only true for him'. And so we get a paradox, of which the limbs are: the equation is simply true, and: the equation is only true for him. This paradox is, in our minds, the symptom of a revelation. Christ is the truth *into which* we have to come.

Christ doesn't tell us and then we see. Christ tells us, haunts us, invades us, takes us over, and *then* we see – in him.

And thus the 'answer' to the humanist is not that we need religion as well as morality, but that we need Christ to equate in us religion and morality. Of course if the humanist replies that this juggling is unnecessary, since we simply don't need religion at all, the answer is that morality will never refill the void left by religion *until* we are in a position really to assert that love is the whole meaning of life. And this is the Christ-position, in which religion and morality are identical.

The love you have for the others will either encounter a prudential limit or it will begin trying to make the universe talk to you in accents you as a man must want to hear. It will seek to be the grammar of a totally transfigured existence.

Life thus meaningful, life meaningful as love, life unfolding *itself* in the love of the brethren as it unfolds in the flowers and the exploding galaxies, is eternal life. (*Note*: It is in this context that Christ makes his final gesture and testament: Eat this: it's me.)

Finally, it is absolutely integral to Christ's message, to this new and unanswerable simplicity, that 'now the time has come'. It is the enthusiasm not merely of a human simplification but of a human arrival. It announces an achievement and immediately evokes a history. For to say that this equation is what man is made for means that this is what man has been growing towards.

In a world of dreams and gods, Israel miraculously became committed to the equation, though necessarily in an imperfect manner, equating religion with morality via the concept of obedience. And to make the equation on those terms is to make its context provincial or sectarian. *This* people believed that *their* way of life was the expression of God's will and *therefore* religious as well as moral. It is only with Christ, the fine flower of Israel, that the equation is made absolute and so universal.

Transfiguration

This is the transfiguration when the stars
articulate the love of man for man
nature transparent to the eye of love
as the new words echo in the shining rocks
and hammer on the tombs: the Christ is here.

What is there new in love? All the world knows
all about love: the newness is that love
is all there is to know about the world.

The captive soul of man
strains after comfort in two directions:

in love he learns that he is not alone
in being alone: and then, alone, he ventures
into the friendless universe of being
and seeks appeasement in God knows how many curious ways.
And this is darkness, this is the human darkness,
this is the very measure of our darkness,
love and religion the two dimensions of darkness.
This is precisely what it is to be in the dark,
and that is why to love your brother in Christ
is precisely what it is to be in the light.
To love your brother in a world that yields
to words that have been said over and over again
only to echo back from the flaming walls of this world.
How have they yielded? Why? Who ever said that there was an
Open Sesame?
There's nothing new in what he says, yet what he says changes
the world.

What is the passion that gave the world away,
laid all its riches bare to any Peter, James or John
who has caught a spark off that fire?
Why, why, why is it true what he says:
love, and the perplexities of 'is' and 'ought'
are walls of paper in a children's maze?
We cannot account for this. But this we know,
That it sends us back to the very beginnings.
It is the dumb beginning of us,
that asks no question,
that betrays itself in questions.
It is this original dumbness of us
that stirs with the awakening rocks
and wells up into an overflow of time
as this man speaks and spells the world out now.

Now now now, it is Christ's Now
rings round the world
and shakes its tombs to yield their dust to joy.
('Lazarus, come forth!' was but a casual aside)

Every man dreams a Now that the world had awaited,
every soul is all time at the flood.
Beware the dream, my soul, beware the voices
that say to it 'he is here' or 'he is there'
and so the Now is lost in here and there,
and then becomes but Then.
But beware also of those who say there is no flood,
no word, no now for ever; for these too
are lost, utterly lost, adrift from the dumb certainty of growing
which has no answer to incarnate word
but to arise and walk a world made new in love.
At last there came a man who said 'at last'
and was the last and found a voice that carried
through all the layers of human expectation
through all the noise of battle and debate
to where the soul is dumb but for one word
and that word Yes, which wakes the universe.

12

Eternal
Life (2)

CHRIST SUCCEEDED IN MAKING HIS POINT OF VIEW
about life and the world prevail over our point of view, not
by rhetoric or any of the normal forces of persuasion, but 'by
himself'. For the forces of persuasion, once they are spent,
allow the previous pattern to re-establish itself. In the case of
Christ we have a unique form of 'persuasion'. It is *like* what
happens when an error in our viewpoint is shown to us,
and our mind reassembles around the truth that we have
not seen. But it is *unlike* this process in that the truth that
takes us over is not a correct proposition but a person: and
this, though it is *like* coming under the sway of a powerful
personality, is *unlike* this latter process in that it has about
it the total and irrevocable finality that characterizes the grasp
of a correct proposition.

By an inexorable logic, inbuilt into the whole situation of
Christ's impact on people, the weight of the argument falls
more and more on Christ himself. Hence the characteristic
Christ-saying is 'I am the truth', 'I am the way, the life', and

the *ego eimi* sayings generally. It is probable that Christ himself never put it that way: rather, like the good teacher he was, he allowed the equation of himself with truth gradually to emerge from the developing confrontation. The *ego eimi* sayings, which mostly appear in the fourth, theological gospel, are statements of Christ's *nature* rather than indications of his *character*.

Notice that it is not fundamentally a case of Christ saying 'this is a love-world' and the disciples accepting this otherwise impossible proposition 'because they admired him so much'. No amount of personal charm, nothing that is in the order of personal influence, can account for the revolution that Christ effected. What happened was, that two world-views came into collision, and the 'love-world' prevailed *in the person of Christ*. In other words, he *was* that world, he was the *whole* world re-centred. What the apostles saw at the Trans-figuration was only a visually hotted-up version of what confronted them in the dusty weather-worn preacher. In describing his impact, all the categories of psychology fail us, and we are constrained to talk of the breaking-in of a new world. The only thing that effectively contradicted the wisdom of man was that parcel of flesh and blood. The more his words became *unanswerable*, the more they became *himself*. (All down the ages, the people we call saints have, in spite of sometimes disturbing kinks and neuroses, in spite of the silly ideas they had picked up, basically said *two* things and meant one thing: said 'love, love, love, only people matter, etc.' and 'him, him, him'. The satanic travesty of this is when 'him, him, him' is hammered at people not by the lover but by the Inquisitor, the torturer, the crusader.)

We have to think, then, of an 'argument' between Christ's Body and the world, both conceived of in their totality, physical and spiritual. The theme of the argument is that each claims to be *the* world. Whichever wins *is the* world. Whichever loses is dispossessed and taken over by the other. Christ won. But since all he had to argue with was *himself*, his normal human vulnerable self, he could only achieve this victory by being destroyed by a force that was immeasurably his superior on the field on which he was compelled to pitch the battle, and prevailing in that very act, revealing his enduring reality and power in a death whose obverse was resurrection. The risen Christ is the new world, the now *only* world, revealed in power and glory and annexing the now dispossessed world, slowly in the nature of the case, but triumphantly, joyously, containing total victory in every moment of Christian life.

In the collision of the rival claimants to be *the* world, Christ was the victor but also, necessarily, the victim. His message put him at the centre, to be destroyed and to prevail.

The only *possible* resolution of the contradiction between Christ's version of the world and our version is in Christ's own self, his body, him. The whole battle over God's truth and our truth necessarily centres on him, in his flesh, and crucifies him. Man says to Christ, 'O.K., so you say the world is this way, which means that you *are* "the world this way". All right, become such a transfigured world. Your only argument is your own flesh which we shall destroy. You have got to make of this destruction the first stage of your argument. The only *conclusive* argument is "you, prevailing in death".' The arrest, passion, death and resurrection of Jesus is God's argument with this world, God getting the truth out of this world by a syllogism of flesh and blood.

Now, once we've got this picture straight, we are in a position to understand all the Christian statements about the 'last things'. It becomes surprisingly simple. There is only one 'last thing': the new world, the transfigured, God-centred world whose law is love, which is the Body of Christ in its full achievement. Now the achieved Christ is the obverse of the dead Christ, the victor the obverse of the victim. And this 'dying into wholeness' is the law of the new world, the manner of its prevailing. The Christian dies into the whole-ness with every creative (that is, death-recognizing) moment of Christian life. This 'dying' is not some esoteric mystical process about which the unbeliever would understand nothing, but is the surrender that a fully conscious human life demands. He 'dies daily' whose responses are organized round that sense of the absurdity of 'myself-as-my-own-world' which would if asked become articulate as a realistic as opposed to an unrealistic view of 'my death'. He who dies daily knows what death really is. Finally, death itself is the final 'dying into the whole'.

This means that the death of a man is the particular 'moment' that he is in the coming of the single new world in Christ, and is a matter of supreme moment, full of personal responsibility for that very reason. The Church, knowing this, has insisted on a particular judgment and its consequences. Further, following a sound instinct, she has recognized the high probability that death for a given man will not be all that it would be were he a totally committed Christian, and has as it were extended the dying process in a doctrine of purgation.

Unfortunately, in default of a live, necessarily contemp-orary, theological synthesis – one which throws the Christian light on man as he now feels himself to be – the habit has grown up of regarding the particularities of this situation as being, in their sum, the whole of it, so that orthodoxy has seemed to demand a type of personal survival that has the properties of individual isolation as we know it: which is the *negation* of the *Christian* doctrine of immortality. A doctrine of immortality that is not, in the first place and as an inclusive and normative proposition, the statement that the other side of death (N.B. not '*on* the other side') is a new world that is this present world transformed in Christ, is not the Christian statement. That the person himself survives in the new world is implicit in the latter's nature as a fully achieved community. It may be inferred from the fact that the more perfect and unified a community, the more do persons as such flourish in it. *How* the person survives we do not know. The classical Christian statement here is: 'Dearly beloved, we are now the sons of God, and it has not been revealed what we *shall* be.'

This huge negative, implicit in the immensely *positive* Christian statement, implicit in the whole Christian law of dissolution as the 'place' of God's appearing, requires not a qualification of the 'agnosticism' in which mortal man confronts death, but on the contrary its full acceptance through the transforming categories of faith, hope and love. What has gone seriously wrong is that the 'Christian negative' has been mitigated, to the fatal detriment of the 'Christian positive'. And thus there has grown up the notion of a lot of parallel lines persisting through death into an endless prolongation as parallel lines. And although a little philosophical reflection will reveal that an after-life cannot be *imagined*, it has become almost the hallmark of orthodoxy to make such an imaginative essay. Certainly the stout *negation* of such a possibility has been no predominant part of the Christian preaching of immortality in this latter age, as it should have been.

As a result, the current Christian notion of 'survival' is itself taking on the unmistakable properties of a survival. Christians are become like an old social order, no longer unified and convinced of itself as part of human life, but counting its now multiple and hence meaningless assets. And the Gallup poll question 'Do you believe in an after-life?' has become, like 'Do you believe in a personal God?' a question that no longer tests a real religious commitment but may reduce to no more than 'Are you a square?'

On this question of *imagining*, there is probably a rather serious epistemological muddle, which can be found at many other points in our received theology. For thomists are fond of saying: 'Not being able to imagine something is not at all the same thing as not being able to conceive it. We can't imagine life after death, but we can and must conceive it.' This grossly oversimplified version of the important difference between imagining and conceiving has led to the notion that we can accept as real a purely logical construct whose formation owes nothing essentially to the imagination. Once we have succeeded in deceiving our minds in this way, we find ourselves assenting to all sorts of propositions as being descriptive of the real. Then, paradoxically but inevitably, the imagination that has been simply *excluded* intrudes in a crude way by reifying, as it were solidifying, the allegedly pure logical construct. The authentic thomist espistemology asserts that the ground of all conceptualization is a dynamic insight into an image. The image is the springboard of intelligence, not a thing to lean back on. Where there has been no image there is no act of intelligence and so the mind is *confined* to the imagination however much this be denied in a particular case. For the understanding of Christian immortality, the requisite images are those that we form in our attempt to understand the Christian fact and the Christian life: of dissolution, of evolution, of the Body of Christ. The immortal condition itself cannot be imagined, but its earthly bases can and must, for it to be conceived. Here, as with the Christian understanding of God with which it is most closely connected, the strength of the Christian Thing lies in the fact that the grounding images correspond to realities that properly are material, to an event that actually has happened and does happen, so that the mind is powerfully launched into a mystery which transcends imagination, and, *qua* mystery, breaks the bounds of thought.

The present weakness of the Christian mind shows itself in the way that Teilhard de Chardin is generally judged to have blurred the awful Christian choices in his evolutionary treatment of the final convergence of all in Christ. In the first place, the evolutionary concept is regarded as univocal and so involving throughout the process a uniform determinatism which, when it gets to the human level, eliminates free-will; whereas in the Teilhardian position the free person is the richest form of the complexity and manifold possibility that is found increasingly as we ascend the scale. More seriously, however, it is assumed that any account of immortality that does not feature *in the first place* the surviving individual is unorthodox: whereas orthodoxy really demands that 'the whole' be the basic concept, and that oneness and immortality be understood as implying each other in our account of man's end. The bread that all men desire to make them immortal is the communion of saints, as Augustine says (Tract 26 *In Joannem*).

I shall die. I shall be judged. But my death is a 'moment', a part, of that final regeneration in which the world is made new in Christ. Neither the contrast between the particularity of death (and the spatial and temporal spread-out-ness of deaths) and the oneness of the end, nor the possibility of individual failure to measure up entirely or at all to the requirements of life and death, militate against this basic proposition. That this makes impossible a detailed map of the next world is not a weakness in the Teilhardian position but a necessary part of the Christian mystery and commitment.

13

On the
Death Bit

THE GREAT TASK OF THE CHRISTIAN TODAY IS TO find, in himself and in the whole world-life of which he is part, the real and exact association of God with death. Death accepted, death-taken-into-yourself, is the condition for God to be real to you. Conversely God, a real initiating and saving God, is the condition for this integration-with-death to take place. It is only in a saving context that the gay world of electrons and stars and politicians can be at once the polished mirror of your death and the dark embrace waiting to receive and destroy you. Only for the Christian is there a real looking-glass land.

That world you look out on will continue unchanged when you are dead. It will print your obituary card and watch it grow yellow. So if you want to see 'yourself dead and gone', just take a look at that world as it goes its way. As far as it is concerned, you are dead already. On the other hand, as far as *you* are concerned, your end will be *its* end. So you are at cross-purposes, you my friend and the world your inseparable mate. The relations between you and it are reproduced, alas, in most of what you optimistically call your personal relationships: for most of your friends are, to you, if you are honest, just bits of world. And the rigidity between you, the perpetual at-loggerheads of two unyielding parties, also is what we mean by death.

What Christ is on about, whether he is telling you to lose your life if you would find it, or whether he is announcing his own death as the centre of his message, is simply the transformation of this at-loggerheads confrontation into a love-affair that is the growing-point.

And if you have been accorded that most precious gift, a happy sexual consummation, do not express this in a hatred of death, for this is to deny God. And do not love death either, for that too is ungodly. Between and above the hatred and the love of death there stands but one thing: the love of Christ who, dead and living, fills this darkness with God.

E

14

The Encapsulated Condition

THE CHRISTIAN MIND IS OPEN TO ALL HUMAN EX-
perience, exposed to death as the abiding human reality, and
knows God as liberation and light in this context of human
insolvency.

But it is already inaccurate to talk of 'the Christian mind'
as such, for such talk ignores the historical dimension which
is essential to Christianity. Similarly, to talk of 'all human
experience' is to imply that all human experience may be
had at any one time.

Thus the above definition is only a broad hint for understanding what has to be situated in one time or place. It
is a reminder of the larger dimensions that open out for the
Christian from any moment in Christian history.

In fact this dual orientation of the Christian mind to an
invading death and to a saving God has always to be realized
in terms of the *sort* of human experience to which people are
open at a particular time. The saving power of God can never
perhaps be entirely dissociated from the way in which man at

a given time tends to save *himself*, to find his life meaningful, to create symbols of wholeness and salvation. Now each 'Christian period' has two limitations. In the first place, its *human* salvation or ennoblement symbols are inadequate to the reality they convey, for they mitigate the sheer transcend- ance of the saving power. In the second place, the symbols lose even the power they originally had when they are carried over, with the attitudes they enshrine, into a subsequent age. Thus for instance the feeling for Christ's poor that came with Francis soon took on a romantic note, which jars when we look at destitution today, in for instance people who have to sleep in public lavatories because they have not that minimum of social viability that is required by the hostel. This is a type of human misery of which medieval man could not be conscious even in kissing the feet of lepers.

Now it seems that what we are suffering from today is a situation in which this phenomenon of carry-over has come to a head, thus creating a completely paradoxical situation. The inherited Christian attitudes become not merely in- adequate to our Christian experience but positively militate against it. The purely this-worldly element in the symbol of salvation becomes all that is left, and so the attitude becomes one of deriving security from an idol instead of the uncreated Grace. The Christian mind shuts itself off from the now- invading world, and seeks a type of security that the more conscious spirits of the time see clearly to be unworthy of man: so that these latter really *represent* the Christian attitude, in which they do not believe, against the traditional believers who do. The saving power, then, is no longer the infinite incomprehensible God, but an *encapsulated* God who offers comfort to the *encapsulated* Christian.

This situation is paralleled in contemporary art and philosophy, where a feeling of the 'monumental' look of these arts as traditionally practised provokes an anti-art and an anti-philosophy. Presumably, then, there is need today, among committed Christians, for an anti-Christianity, or at least for the recognition that those who now find Christian belief difficult or irrelevant are not necessarily weakening in their Christian faith.

St John of the Cross said that if you suffered a distaste for spiritual things you were either lazy or entering on the dark night of the soul. In addition to these alternatives there is a third possibility, which he would only have understood to the extent of saying: 'You haven't found the "right" spiritual book.' But today this third possibility has been immensely enlarged. It is that you may be sufficiently conscious as a human being living in this time to feel that *all* the available spiritual literature is offering a spiritual attitude that is hallowed only by time. I think that this condition is becoming increasingly general, and that we are approaching a point where those who do not suffer from it are estranged, by this very fact, from the life which is trying to find a voice in the Church of today.

15

Does God break in?

NO, HE BREAKS OUT, NOT IN THE SPATIAL SENSE that the above question bears, but rather in the sense of an epidemic.

There is a serious danger that the new movements – biblical, liturgical, catechetical, and even ecumenical – may come to inhibit the speculative and God-seeking mind more than did the old scholasticism. While the latter sought to preserve the essentially gratuitous shape of the Christian fact by insisting on certain *propositions*, our 'new' orthodoxy tends to compass this end by insisting on a certain *picture*. And while it is true that there is no thinking without pictures, to *tie* the mind to a picture is to reverse the mind's dynamic which is to bounce *off* pictures into insight.

The picture which replaces the old propositions is of God *dramatically breaking into human history*. But the true and perennial balance of Christian belief is found by not stating the divine Advent in the 'realist' language of 'breaking-in', and by realizing the gratuitous nature of this Advent in terms of the community which it alone and uniquely brings into being. It is the seriousness of our understanding of, and commitment to, the community that is Christ risen and ever-growing, that allows the God-fact, the Advent, to deploy in the Church the meaning which cannot be described in itself. This balance has for me that extraordinary force that the facts are found to have when they are apprehended in their own native arrangement. It's like discovering the 'facts of life' – one of those moments in which the understanding of some specific matter comes upon us as a sudden increment in self-understanding. It puts us in accord with the more intelligent scholastic theologian who, knowing how the mind works, rightly insists that an existential picture can never *replace* an abstract formula, and that however arid scholastic formulas may have been, they at least did not put the mind in the way of trying to *imagine* the truth they sought to convey. This newly-discovered balance of Christian truth opens the way to an orthodoxy that is at once sympathetic with the best of the scholastic tradition and is itself a post-progressive radicalism.

In this balance we approach a point of crisis, where the teacher begins to realize that his *understanding* of the Christian fact, of the God-fact, is his easy, open, completeness-seeking, humble relation to the community. It is the end of the mono-logian. It is the painful human crisis of the teacher himself, both as teacher and as believer. It is the truth declared by Paul when he said: '*You* are our message, written not in ink on paper but in the fleshy tables of the heart.'

And only now perhaps do the essential qualities of a valid concept-for-God show themselves. A valid God-concept differs from all other concepts, of God or of anything else, in that it embodies a further dimension, namely the act of mutual understanding in which alone it can be embraced. It as it were anticipates that embrace. It is therefore necessarily incomplete or rather uncompleted, open-ended. Such a concept is open to people. It invites the hearer's response, and awaits it as an increment in its own validity.

The valid religious teacher is he who is engaged on a venture with those he converses with, is carrying on the dialogue and mutual searching that is described in the gospels. The valid God-concept differs from the fixed conventional God-concept not by its subtlety or abstruseness, but by the seriousness with which it takes the hearer; not only by what it tells him but by what it asks him and asks of him. It requires in him no expertise except the expertise of real living.

This concept seeks a community, wants to *be* a community meshed in mutual acceptance, understanding and enrichment. It eschews finality, not in the agnostic or political spirit for which all formulas are provisional, but simply because the community that shares and enlarges it is ever incomplete, ever growing in depth and in coverage of the human spectrum.

Today the validity of the concept and the reality of the commitment it expresses and asks for are converging. There is a rapidly growing sense of hollowness about even a brilliantly articulated Christian doctrine of God unaccompanied by, or at least separable from, human commitment. And human commitment is commitment of persons to persons. This new awareness of the real issues profoundly questions the division between progressives and conservatives as an adequate analysis of controversy in the Church. For from this point of view, the progressive can be profoundly closed and the conservative surprisingly open.

For a long time the more penetrating and independent spirits, like Dostoevsky, have seen the validity of Christian belief in just these terms. If the preacher, they said, has nothing to say to the man whom suffering has brought to the edge of meaning: if his teaching does not urge him out into the terrifying twilit world where man must, it seems, despair of meaning, his belief is at least in some doubt. These thoughts are becoming disturbingly relevant today, not merely in relation to the meeting of individuals at the human frontier, but as a comment on the Church itself. As laying down the condition for sacramental validity, such an idea is obviously silly. But as describing the condition in which alone the Church can commend her sacramental treasures and look for fruit from them, it is profoundly true.

And only now a correlation occurs to me which may be what this book has been looking for: between the dynamic transcendence of God over all man's concepts of God, and the manner in which God is known in the Christian community: between the cloud of unknowing and the cloud of witnesses. The former of these two correlates is not specifically Christian, although the certainty of Christian faith has given to this ascent of the mind to the unknown an urgency and conviction that it could not otherwise have. 'This unknown God that you worship, we make known to you.' It has prevented the mystic's 'uncertainty *what*' from falling back into an 'uncertainty *that*'. (Thus for instance the agnostic Matthew Arnold *says* that all religious creeds are but attempts to express the inexpressible, and it is difficult to quarrel with him. But his thoughts are not *dominated* by the importance of this inexpressible reality, so that the phrase 'to express the inexpressible' is little more than a fine phrase. He is not, as Nietzsche was, a God-persecuted man. He is a cultured gentleman, a taster of philosophies and religions.)

But the Christian faith mates with the mystic unknowing in another and far more intimate way. For not only does it make certain the *object* of the unknowing, it also profoundly transforms the unknowing itself. The experience of the solitary mystic constantly passing beyond images in search of the light gives way to the holy community for ever re-

discovering God in its evolving pattern of mutual understanding, and thus for ever confessing him anew as the mystery
in its midst. The community, like the solitary mystic, knows
that no stage of the ascent is final: but, unlike him, it knows
from present experience that the final vision will be a
coalescence of people in perfect oneness of heart and mind.
It lives in the knowledge of enfleshed mystery, an enfleshed
transcendence. The stages that mark the solitary mystic's
progress are *images* in his mind. The stages that mark the
community's growth in God are *real people* in their growing
concord and mutually given love and daring. The passing
from image to image to perfect light of which Paul speaks is
the growing perfection of the *community*, of the *ecclesia*, as
image of God, as concorporate with the Son. This coalescent
process deploys not only the conscious growth of the holy
community but also the great shifts and movements of socially
developing man. And although my point of view here is not
specifically the Teilhardian, the resemblance my conclusion
bears to Teilhard is striking. Perhaps Teilhard himself did not
realize the extent to which his vision is corroborated by the
Christian tradition's specific transformation of moral,
religious and mystical man. Perhaps those who think Teilhard
engrafts a new religion on to Christianity have themselves
failed to take that next step into the fulness of Christian
understanding which is opening up in our time.

We can now understand more adequately the phenomenon
of the 'encapsulated condition' already noted. For the once
potent Christian symbols that are now become obstacles are
precisely those emblems in which, from time to time, the
holy community's self-understanding crystallizes: the monk,
the knight, the consecrated monarch, the Pontifex Maximus,
and so on. In that world, men bound themselves together in
Christ and found him in the very symbols with which they
did this – in oil, in crown, in accolade. And we who 'know

only a heap of broken images where the sun beats' have to find him anew. Tradition does not furnish us with the symbols we need, but it does tell us where they are to be sought – in the life of the community. It is interesting to note in this context that even modern Christian movements, such as the Young Christian Workers, have enrolment ceremonies that evoke, as Christian, the medieval symbolism of investiture. Of course the new symbols cannot be thought up. They emanate only from life, and this only when life has become intensely felt together in a particular way at a particular time. The current absence of Christian symbols is due less to the lack of poetry and the weakness of the Christian imagination than to the failure to discover afresh and in daringly new accents the life of Christ in us as men and women of today. A false notion of orthodoxy still diverts us from the holy thing that is happening now to the immobilized forms of a vanished Christian culture. And as all the indications are that we are being called upon to live much more *consciously* the drama of the human community than was demanded of the preceding Christian generations, it would seem that we have to achieve consciously the common life whence may eventually emerge the symbols of a new Christian age: and this means that we in the interim must learn to live *without* symbols. This is difficult to achieve, for the human unity that is lived without symbols too easily gets watered down to the vague abstract aspirations that are nowadays on the lips of our statesmen. Nevertheless there is no escaping the task. The Christian options at the present time are well expressed in the following conclusion to a recent study of the modernist crisis: 'It is, indeed, quite true that vague religiosity is of no use to mankind. But it is also true that there are men – and those the best, perhaps, of our kind – who are determined to live without idols' (John Crean in *Continuum*, Summer 1965, p. 151). When Tennyson wrote 'Ring in the Christ that is to be' he was doubtless giving expression to the shallow philosophy of his age. Nevertheless those words bear a Christian sense that we in our age cannot afford to ignore.

Let me return at last to the stated subject of this chapter by saying that the dominant symbol of our redemption, especially among liturgical and catechetical progressives, is the image of 'God breaking in'. For the Christian community has still to rise to the awful challenge, so inadequately though so courageously met by the modernists and in our time by the Bishop of Woolwich, of conceiving of the new life in Christ simply as a life that has come to be in us as men and women, while maintaining with the strictest orthodoxy the gratuitous and gracious nature of the divine initiative that has brought this life into being. We must learn to say to our time and of ourselves in this time: 'We know that we have passed from death to life, *because* we love the brethren.'

16

Jesus Christ Yesterday
– and Today?

CHRIST IS THE REFULGENT IMAGE OF THE FATHER, but in this dark, slowly and erratically unfolding world Christ himself has many images. The orthodox statement of his nature has been hammered out in abstract propositions of enduring truth, but the process whereby he comes into the minds of men is vastly more complicated, temporally conditioned, and erratic. Nevertheless it is this latter process and its varying results that is of crucial moment. To it the scientific theologian is as subject as is the unlettered believer.

The question that the human mind perforce puts to itself when it tries to accommodate Christ is something like this: Given the basic supposition of orthodox dogma that Christ has an *official* role in the world of men, how shall we describe that role by comparison with official roles as we know them? Tradition came to select three of these roles and to see them wonderfully blended and unified in the Christ: King, priest, and prophet.

Now, in this process of enrolling Christ in the human

community, an interesting dialectic is observable. For although each of the above-mentioned roles is meaningless except as applied to a member of the community and so does not suggest an outsider, the attempt to construct the image of Christ in terms of human roles tends to just this conclusion. For we are trying to convey the uniqueness and transcendence of Christ in terms of human status, and the only category that human status language knows for the transcendent is *the distant*. It is only in the pure detached language of scientific theology that the divinity of Christ does not swamp the humanity and that the humanity maintains its meaning as the one-of-us-ness of Christ. Theological language is able to maintain this balance only because it knows nothing of the world of men as they actually live together, bear rule and are governed. The moment we try to translate the theological picture of Christ into the language of that world, the latter must furnish for it the only concept it knows for transcendence, that of sovereignty.

Let us try another angle. The priest, the prophet, and the king have their roles *in a particular community*. The members of the community take on a subject role *as members of this community*, not simply *as men*. As men they remain the equals of princes and priests. What we have is the organization of a part of the human family for a specific purpose, and the differentiations of status are meaningful only in relation to this part and this purpose. Widen the picture to the human whole, and the differentials disappear, so that even in a feudal age it becomes a commonplace that death is 'the beggar's nurse and Caesar's'. But when, as with Christ, the community ruled and served *is* the whole human family, then humanity ceases to equalize what society has differentiated. For humanity itself is what is involved. And so it is precisely *as men* that all are *under* Christ. Hence an image of Christ as more than man, as above man. (I am not referring to the strictly theological 'more than man', but to a sort of V.I.P. concept which naturally forms in people's minds and is in practice more influential than the theology of the business.)

In this image, Christ *as man* is distanced from the human community, to which he comes as the representative of a higher Power. The theological statement that God sent his Son has been accommodated by the double fiction of considering the whole human race as a community and imagining relations between this community and a foreign power.

This imbalance was always being corrected under the pressure of the Christian fact, but never totally. The correcting process never really penetrated and transformed the regal image. It managed to suggest the mysterious and surprising truth only by the artistic device of paradox: the jewelled conceit of the universal King reigning from the Tree. The manner of Christ's reigning, dispensing with the trappings of royalty and adopting instead the degradation of the Cross, was thought of in terms of the extraordinary condescension that characterises the really great, rather than in its own mysterious terms.

It is a golden rule that a thought that *rests* on paradox has not really broken through to the truth of things. The paradoxical talk of Christ is strictly a means to an end, to surprise the mind out of its conventional postures in order to prepare it for the single truth of God. Do we really see that Paul's statement that God has chosen the weak things of this world to confound the strong insinuates a metaphysical reality? Don't we think of it rather in a sort of half-resolved way? And has not Christian tradition positively abounded in this sort of moralistic, half-worked-out concept of humility? Nietzsche rightly complained that Christians have used the gospel to exalt human mediocrity over the really excellent, judging the latter to be proud. (The only other way in which the gap has been closed has been a uniquely horrible sentimentalism, productive of a uniquely horrible art. We have passed from the regal humanity of the Byzantine Christ to the hermaphroditic humanity of the holy picture.) The real message of the crib is that man is heir to the universe. Seeing this is a breakthrough from the disguised Foreign Prince of Christian myth to the Man of Christian faith.

Have we ever really understood this? Have we really clothed the Christian mystery in its own flesh which is our flesh? Have we not set it in terms of the game that men play this side of death, injecting ritual meaning into a life which cannot reveal its meaning in this gay half-world of the half-alive, the not yet dead? And does not the humanity of Christ, claiming meaning throughout the human spectrum and so tearing down all our securities, coining a new human royalty, still await our slow understanding? Have we yet really felt the texture of the flesh that is given us as our food, the blood our drink?

Of course there is an unorthodox Christian reaction to the feudalized Christian mystery. It is that which sees Christ as the revolutionary, abolishing religion and all the ceremonial trappings of man, and laying bare the human fact. This appears powerfully in *The Grand Inquisitor* and passim in the works of Dostoevsky, and again in the 'religionless Christianity' currently fashionable. Paradoxically it bids fair to burden wretched man with yet another religion. Yet it is surely an element in the solution, the really human vesture of the mystery, taken off the mystery and hung out on the line. And most orthodox Christian criticism of this new Christianity fails to appreciate the real issues, fails to look forward to the point when the whole mystery of God will be known in the clasp of your brother's hand.

17

The New Orthodoxy
– Semi-existentialism

ENTHUSIASTS FOR SALVATION-HISTORY TEND TO assume that it is a substitute for the conceptual framework of scholastic theology. They rightly say it is an improvement on the latter; but we can't leave the matter there. We must be more precise about the nature of this 'improvement'. Do we mean that *what was once done* by the communication and explication of concepts can now be done, and better done, by talking about salvation-history? It seems that this is implied, mistakenly in my view.

Now I am not pleading for the old, conceptual approach, nor even considering the respective *merits* of the two approaches, but simply examining the proposition that *what* the old method did the new method can do.

What is this 'what'? It is that conveying of knowledge in which the thing imparted is contained in what is said, in such a way that the interpersonal situation of teacher and taught does not enter formally and substantially into the matter. Of course this situation enters *in some way* into all teaching.

THE NEW ORTHODOXY—SEMI-EXISTENTIALISM · 143

A boring, humourless, closed-minded teacher will put over any subject badly. But the point is that the salvation-history approach is treated by some as though it contained the 'riches' of the Christian faith more adequately than the 'conceptual' approach, *apart* from the consideration of the teacher-disciple relationship which is in fact an inhibiting or promoting factor in *either* approach. And this is what I question.

At the grass-roots level, it is not clear that it is good either for a child or for an intelligent adult to be cajoled into looking at the universe through the eyes of an ancient Jew. I am amazed at the naïve enthusiasm with which the producers of the new and brighter missals and the compilers of bible services talk of 'God's mighty deeds'.

At a more philosophical level, the epistemological foundations of the 'new' approach are questionable. It seems to be based on a sort of half-baked existentialism, in which the idea of 'encounter' is accorded the sort of hard currency value given to the idea of grace or the supernatural. The intelligent square justly observes that the new people substitute for, e.g., 'I believe that there are three persons in God', the statement 'I believe in the divine encounter', which is even further removed from the concrete.

But positive examination of the 'new' position makes its weakness really apparent. For 'encounter' is an existential notion. And existential knowledge does not mean having a vivid picture instead of an 'arid' concept. In existential knowledge something is known as an experienced transformation, or better *in* an experienced transformation, in the knower, or as a significant increment in his self-awareness. This is classically expressed in St Augustine's prayer, *noverim te, et noverim me*. To talk of an encounter with God is to refer to a quickening of consciousness, a conscious unfolding in oneself. Anyone who talks of the divine encounter without at least wishing he could write poetry is talking about nothing at all. He is guilty of the supreme conceptualism, offering something apparently alive, which is worse than offering something manifestly dead. He is opening up before the thirsty wanderer the mirage that is the final exacerbation of thirst.

In this matter of God, the guidelines of scripture combine with the deepest experience of the human predicament to suggest that the above 'quickening' is: a new and exciting sense of my mortality as something that pervades all my experience, suggests a terrifying act of self-surrender, in-augurates a peculiar dialogue with the universe of which I am part, illuminates my sexual awareness of myself and others, and could be 'talked from' to young people who never think of death but experience in a painful and meaning-seeking form the identity-crisis which is our mortal lot. Yes, all this and a great deal more.

Ultimately, there are only two sorts of knowing. (This is a simplification for the sake of clarity.) First, the knowing in which I aim at a hard conceptual structure in which contra-dictions are detected and ruthlessly eliminated, however much I feel that in so doing I am losing the richness of an experience. Second, the quite other sort of knowing for which this richness is all-important: I grope for forms of self-expression to accommodate it and am dangerously delighted when someone else seems to catch on. Now it is impossible to do both these activities at once, and there is nothing in between.

In trying to talk about knowing I am obviously talking of communication. We have come to appreciate how inseparable these two are. Thus in stressing the subjective in existential knowing – or rather in simply stressing existential knowing – one is equivalently asserting that the communication of this knowledge will be an opening of oneself to another person. The paradigm here will be sexual union, traditionally described as a mutual knowing. It is this *kind* of thing, this kind of personal world, that one is opting for whether one likes it or not in seeking to existentialize Christian doctrine and instruction. To talk of existentializing, and still to think primarily in terms of a text-book, even the Bible – nay, especially the Bible, *corruptio optimi pessima* – is to enter on a way that is intellectually incoherent and personally frustrating for teacher and disciple alike. Thinking in text-book terms means thinking that it is *this*, these words, that we, teacher and disciple, are aiming to understand. No, it is *ourselves* that we are aiming to understand, ourselves as Christians, ourselves as the 'disjecta membra' of the universe, become in Christ the members of one body. We strive to exist, to ourselves and to each other, as members of Christ. We see each other as a real and significant increment to our understanding of Christ and of the Christian Thing.

The poverty of our Christian instruction, and the poverty of our common life, was at first thought to consist in the inadequacy of the *content* of our teaching. The remedy was thought to lie in 'getting back to the Bible'. It doesn't. It consists in getting back to ourselves. 'Back to the Bible' was all right, however, as a first stage. For man never hits a bull's eye first go in the matter of diagnosing his ailments. First comes the approximation, the attempt to cure the symptoms. And this is good, for it takes us a step nearer to the malady, building up the crisis in which the real step will be clear and forced upon us. That crisis is now upon the Church, as she moves away from a purely theoretical knowledge which makes a kind of sense while remaining purely theoretical, to the world of the Bible that makes no such sense. For the Bible is the plan of a city where men meet, know each other at last in the transforming Spirit, and love, and sing together those psalms, hymns and spiritual canticles of which Paul speaks and which are not a liturgist's or a choirmaster's problem.

18

Gathering
the Threads

THE PROPOSITION THAT IS CLOSEST TO THE VERY
centre of our common faith is that he who loses his life shall
save it. It applies not only to the material dispositions of our
egoism, but to the spiritual universe we construct to secure
ourselves against uncertainty.

The anatomy of this construction is a subtle and unobserv-
able transmutation of the very propositions that enunciate
our liberation, so that they come to encase and protect our
unwillingness to die. In their original form, the Christian
statements about Christ and grace are as it were shafts of light,
which far from removing or dealing with the surrounding
darkness, accept the necessity of leaving much in the dark as
the condition of affirming the true light. In this form, the
statements are felt, by the ego which dislikes mystery, to be
insufficient. So they are imperceptibly converted into good
solid descriptions of what reality is actually like. Christ
becomes a sort of amphibian at home in the two worlds,
operating now in his human nature, now in his divine nature,

covering the whole sweep of the universe and taking all the mystery out of it. Grace becomes an asset, storable in the soul apart from the divine and human encounter which is the conscious Christian life from moment to moment. The after-life becomes a survival of ourselves as we know ourselves, which for purely accidental reasons cannot be imagined or described. Concepts become things to hold on to. And thus the Christian way becomes a shelter carved out of this world.

This enterprise comes under the judgment of a sound epistemology, which tells us that the 'realism' that consists in reifying concepts is the way into Cloud Cuckoo Land. It also comes under the judgment of Christian faith itself, which classes these solidified dogmas among the props that the follower of Christ through death and resurrection has to junk.

The process of reification shows itself in the situation created by a divided Christendom. The Great Church which in this confused situation is the home and custodian of Christian certainties, comes to fulfil this function by emphasizing the security that she offers to her fortunate inmates. And thus the Catholic contrasts sharply with his bewildered separated brethren as having his journey through life neatly mapped out. An apologetic is worked out that does not rely on the central Christian proposition of life through death, that eschews as hopelessly vague the apostolic statement that we know we have passed from death to life because we love the brethren, and appeals exclusively to the Petrine claims and to those descriptions of the Church that are concerned with her institutional character.

From this point of view the primary function of the ecumenical movement is to assist the great process of return to the true well-spring of Christian hope. With every sacrifice of those 'Catholic attitudes' that have hardened, through angry confrontation with protestant Christianity, into a travesty of the Christian certainty, a step however small in the direction of that certainty may be taken. *May* be taken, for this process when not under the sway of the Spirit leads to a version of the Christian Thing that savours of the *Reader's Digest*.

But if we say 'under the sway of the Spirit' we must mean it, accepting the fact that the discernment between the true way and the false is of the Spirit alone. We cannot expect to know exactly what the Christian options are at each moment. Our only principle is an inner and basic fidelity, extraordinarily difficult to achieve without leaning on the attitudes to which we were brought up.

We have to become much more certain of the Resurrection than we have been, and this means a certainty that the Spirit is working this change in the world at this moment. For in this old mind of ours the Resurrection too can become old. We must be ever searching for that central Christian insight in which the Resurrection establishes itself as at once the basic Christian concept, the supremely desired human excellence, and a fact. And this search probes the very lineaments of the soul. It has a certain negative check that is becoming especially clearly available to us nowadays: the ability to recognize death in ourselves as the big theme of self-deception. Of course we cannot carry through the search in terms of this negative check, which of itself only shows that self-deception and the evasion of death are convertible terms. But we can push the analysis further. It is not just the *evasion* of death that is convertible with self-deception, as though a non-self-deceptive attitude to death were possible. Our predicament is that all 'attitudes' to death are self-deceptive. The only way out is that carved by God in Christ out of this world, in which we not merely 'accept death' but *die* in Christ.

In the midst of this dead world of my mind, among the monuments in which I see *all* the achievements of men as solidified and so denied, in a world where beautiful things seem to demand for their preservation vulgar compromises, life is a must, a seemingly unattainable must. And the life that *there* declares itself as a must is the life of which Christ speaks to me, the life attained in dying, the life in which we are compounded with our death by the Spirit (as opposed to living our death by our own light), the life that is me and this world no longer playing our game of hide-and-seek but wholly at one.

But this description and commendation of the risen life has about it a radical imperfection: that it is not spoken to you my brother *and* that when it *is* spoken to you it will sound terribly lame. For as I repeat it to you, I am painfully aware that I am not invoking a Person but describing a thing. And this awareness comes upon me just because *you* are a person, and no *thing* can be worthy of you. It is you, and your demand on me, that alerts me to the non-personal nature of this 'risen life' of which I speak. The real point here is that you alert me to the *lie* in what I am offering, which is the fact that it *ought* to be personal and yet isn't. It becomes personal, however, the moment we communicate in it, the moment this 'risen life' ceases to be something that I am holding in myself in contradiction of its nature. This risen-life theorem is precisely the point of intersection of a personal visitation and an interpersonal bond. This 'point' can be in a sense described, involving me in all the complexities of the death-theme. But it cannot, just by this description, come alive.

Dumbly this new life that I strive to commend to you seeks its real vitality. I can *call* it life. I can define it as the life that is a 'must' when we have taken stock of the death in us. Another theology has sought to describe it in terms of a quasi-biological superiority to the life we know. But it is all in vain. It is not convincingly 'life' until it is *his* presence *in us*. The real difficulty of making this 'point' clear, this point where the Christian asserts life and the humanist wonders what he is talking about, is that this is the point where the meaning of the personal God and of our personal bond in him is originally coined.

19

Conclusion
to Part Two

THE GOD OF NEW TESTAMENT TIMES IS ABOVE ALL, and as the whole substance of his revelation, a God experienced and confessed in the life of the community; but the God preached in and by the Church of today is disturbingly detached from what little community-experience we have. The 'this-end' of our Christian preaching is not you and I living in a oneness of faith, hope and love, convinced by the Christ in our midst that this bond of ours is for ever, but a past event, something that has happened to those men and is not happening to us. This difference in pattern places our Christian doctrine today in grave peril of no longer announcing the God of Jesus Christ at all. It is to the faith and experience of other men long dead, and not to our own faith and experience, that we are appealing for our notion of God. Thus we have lost the whole Christian understanding of God. It is this remoteness of God from a shared experience in togetherness that gives to our notion of God a remote, thinkable-apart, circumscribed quality that contradicts his nature and the whole shape of his self-disclosing. A community that ceases to *be* the revelation of God cannot hope to *understand* that revelation, except with the understanding of the historian of religions. And there is in fact disturbingly little difference in atmosphere and accent between the modern theologian and the student of religious origins. There is not that unique and unanswerable savour of resurrection that can only come from a shared experience, a feeling of God in our midst. There is not that sense of the inextricable mutual implication of encountering God and loving one another whence comes the authentic Christian understanding of God. The God of history means one thing when 'history is now and England', our attempt to live together and come to understand a little of what is happening to us, and quite another thing when history is past. It is the difference between an all-pervading present experience and a Being regarded as the principal actor in a drama long past. Such a Being, I submit, is a myth, an ikon, and it is to this idol that our Christian worship is addressed. The loss of Christian contact with the living God is to be accounted for in terms of the weakening of the community. It is the community thus impoverished and deprived of its living God that *then* chooses *instead* the God of the Greco-Roman culture. This God is not he who has lured the community away from its centre but rather he towards whom the community deprived of its centre inevitably drifts. This as against Woolwich's view that the idol simply *supplanted* the God of Jesus Christ.

When our Lord tells us that at the judgment it will be our mutual love that will be the test of whether we have ever *known* him, he is telling us *what God is like*. Are we supposed to ignore this parable, continue to pursue a God of our religious imagining, and learn when it is too late that this God has no existence? Will we ever realize that this imagined God of ours died with Jesus and inaugurated the reign of the living God in Christ's Body the Church?

Not only does our Christian teaching today take little account of the 'experienced human component' without which the content of that teaching becomes a really different thing. We have reached the further point at which any serious attempt to restore the human dimension and refract through it the Christian certainty, thus arriving at an idea of God very different from that to which we have grown accustomed, is regarded as of doubtful orthodoxy. This is indeed a Pickwickian situation, where the most serious attempt to recover the Christian balance is regarded as the upsetting of the balance and thus as heresy. The real sickness is of a community that has come to feel itself less and less of a community: in which all that survives of its mutual gestures are the conventions in which they are ritualized: in which the chasuble and the liturgical kiss are ecclesially meaningful, the spontaneous handshake and the oneness in sexual union are not: a community distrustful of the flesh and forgetful of its recreation: a community from which the God that was once its life and light has receded and hardened into a limiting 'objectivity'. Once we appreciate our situation in these radical terms, we see how tragically inadequate for its remedying are the new movements of which we make so much. The lifeless community puts on the apparent life of an articulate worshipping assembly. The distant God is clothed again in the vivid language of the Bible.

The true reformer is not he who can titillate our jaded palates with novelties that will shock the conventional and rally the discontented to a new orthodoxy. He will bring to our minds things that no one, whatever his theological views, will dare to controvert. He will ask what we think St Paul meant when he said that what proved we were sons of God was the Spirit of God's Son in our hearts crying Abba Father. He will recall to us the stern and strictly theological claim which our brother makes upon us in the plain teaching of Christ.

It is only out of a renewed Christian community that a theology worthy of the name will emerge able to restore that name from its present justly dishonoured position in the minds of men to the honour that properly belongs to it.

PART THREE

Statements

I

Resurrection[1]

I WANT TO EXAMINE THE VERY ROOTS OF CHRISTIAN
unity, to study the community that flashed into being at the
moment when the risen Christ stood among his own. I want
to show that *the concept of religious association* was, in that
moment, radically transformed.

This concept is the concept of 'man dressed out for
celebration'. By a profound necessity inscribed in our unregenerate nature, man has to disguise his common humanity
before he can adopt publicly the posture of prayer. Religion
demands dignity, and dignity demands disguise. And so the
terms on which we come together preclude us from having
quite that sense of mutual exposure that characterizes basic
man, man in the barrack room. We all know some delightful
and colourful characters who would disconcert the religious
assembly if they appeared at a service. I am always amused by
a clause in the levitical regulations that secures the priest
against possible laughter as he mounts the altar steps. Religion
would break down, the author felt, were the congregation to

1. Sermon preached at Liverpool Parish Church for the Unity
Octave, 1966

become suddenly conscious that the priest is an ordinary man.

Now Jesus gathered the apostles into a religious association. They felt each other not so much as men, but rather as Jews whose religion was being made much more meaningful by this exciting new rabbi. But he lifted them right out of this world. Under his touch, Judaism became more than a religion. It overflowed into all life. The wild flowers glowed in it. Still, the fellowship of the disciples, although lit with this new fire, was not adequate to this new situation. Until he is radically transformed, man must needs divide God off from life. And so the new and total vision and single enthusiasm that Jesus communicated was contradicted by the very nature of his devoted followers. Something devastating had to happen. The situation built up a crisis, *the* human crisis. Dark hints were dropped by the Master as to the nature of this crisis and its necessary issue. There was disturbing talk about a shameful death. The evangelists insist very strongly that these hints were not taken. They were not even understood. They were resolutely suppressed out of the idyllic consciousness in which they hung on his other words.

Then it happened. The horror beyond imagining, stunning the heart into a stony deadness. The Master was arrested. No supernatural agencies came to his aid. A hasty trial was followed by a common execution. It was all over. Can you call to mind an experience like that? Perhaps an idyllic happiness, a love that lit up all the world for you, and then suddenly a policeman at the door, looking awkward, trying to find words to tell you, and among his words some word like 'accident' tells you without knowing it. You take it in and you don't take it *on*, for you can't. It's the absurd, the impossible – and it's happened. Thus, it seemed, ended the Jesus-dream. Yes, that's what the brutal facts said to the apostles: it was a dream. It's got to come to an end. The powers that be, the powers that stand for order in this world, the police, the people who stop the kissing, they'll come in and end the dream and restore the normal, unexciting, meaningless round of existence. The world, that seemed to have been charmed into an innocuous stillness by Jesus's words, flowed back in a dark wave of brute fact, stunning these wretched men who had believed.

What had they in common, except to be a bunch of men for whom God was dead, on whom God had died? There was not even religion left. They had seen too much, and they had seen too much go. They were thrown right back on the purely human, King Lear's poor bare forked animal. They had nothing more in common than the soldiers swopping lewd jokes as they waited for the death of the victims. By the death of God – and even the theologians admit that it was exactly that – those men were plunged into that darkest region of our being where God has not meaning and death reigns.

It was in *that* state of human consciousness that they received the shock that is still with us and will be to the end of time when it will blossom into the glory of eternity. In that assembly of spiritually naked men, the dead Master was suddenly present, alive. It was himself, not 'his spirit', or a sudden becoming-vivid of his memory. At the same time, it was something quite new and mysterious. Not one of them thought, even for a moment, 'Good heavens, didn't he die then after all? Did he revive?' This was no revival. This was no survival. This was the Resurrection. This was God gathering all into himself.

In that indivisible moment of time, the Church was born: an association of men not in religion but in God: an association that went to the very roots of human existence where nature meshes us together after her fashion. This assembly, this community, is the whole substance of the gospel. Yes, God help us, we, you and I, are the good news, we the light of the world, we the one hope of the world, the City set on

F

a hill. This community is the centre of Paul's message. Its coming-to-be is so inseparable from the Resurrection itself, it so much *is* the Resurrection, that he can only call it Christ's Body. And a modern theologian has said 'he died an individual and rose a Mystical Body'. A poetic way of putting it, but then the thing itself is a poem, the divine poiesis, the enfleshed Word of God. And the primary task of the Christian community is to show to the world, in all its splendour and in its total humanity, this reality that is the risen Christ. It is a corporate reality, a human togetherness. Its roots go deeper into the human than men normally dare to go. And on the other hand it extends into that other darkness which men also fear, the dark night of God. It unites these two extremities, of the flesh and of the Spirit, in one life. Its emblem is Christian marriage: which, fully realized, loves and affirms the flesh in a manner impossible to the godless, and at the other end grows serenely into the eternal family of God. All this was built up in that indivisible moment when the dead Christ stood alive in the midst of his dejected flock.

The realization of this reality in our midst demands that we abandon *all* in our corporate religious attitudes that smacks of the old pre-Christ world, all stiffness, all churchiness. That we become alive to each other and mutually accepting at the most humble and earthy level, so that the Spirit may build us right up and seat us 'in the heavenly places, in Christ Jesus'.

Compared with this task, all activities directed to the healing of inter-church divisions are secondary. It is their prerequisite, the condition of their being fruitful. It is the actual life and limb and gesture of Christ, which as a matter of course takes those divisions into its sweep. If the full and authentic life of Christ, if the corporate resurrection experience, were realized once again on earth, the reunion of the Churches would happen almost without our knowing it. Theologians will tell us that love is no substitute for facing the facts of dogmatic differences, but I sometimes wonder whether they have not completely forgotten the love, the oneness, that is the sum and substance of all dogma.

While in the matter of Christian reunion in the technical sense, it is not always clear what we should do, in this matter of letting the Spirit of Christ into our communities, it is always painfully clear what we must do. We have to accept one another in Christ, befriend one another in Christ, as the apostle says. This is the new life and – let us make no mistake here – we fall pathetically and desperately short of it even with those with whom we are, as we dare to say, in communion. Too often a technically valid state of community covers over a mutual indifference that is terrifying.

The Resurrection turns this world upside down. Alas, there is little in our lives, little in our community, little in our preaching, that turns the world upside down. The Resurrection joins the flesh to the stars, the kingdom of the dead to the kingdom of God. But most of us live timorously between these two extremes of flesh and spirit. I am absolutely convinced that there has to be such a renewal of the Christian consciousness and conscience as will make our present Christian outlook almost unrecognizable, our present Christian divisions petty and absurd, irrelevant to the thing itself, the giant strides of Christ in this world. The mind of modern man is furnished by science and art with an arsenal of self-knowledge such as man has never had before. He lives in this finely furnished room, yet he is riddled with insecurity and fear, for it is still in the dark. The light has but to be switched on. Let us, the poor little flock of Christ, open our hearts to him. Then we may surprise ourselves as we hear ourselves saying to a darkened world: 'Rise up, you who sleep, and arise from the dead. And Christ shall enlighten you.' May he achieve this will in us, who with the Father in the Spirit is one only God, world without end. Amen.

2

The Recovery of
Christian Experience

FIRST, THE BASIC EXPERIENCE, OF BEING A HUMAN being, of being alive to all around you. Alive to other people, and to all the different ways in which you relate to them. Alive, confusedly, to the whole world at this present time. Alive to the passage of time, to the unfolding of your life and of the lives of those in whom you are interested. Alive, vaguely, to the fact that you will die. Alive, perhaps, to the fact that death is now: a presence of death whose sign is the anomalous nature of all experience. All these bearings intersect in you, and your consciousness gives a sense of unity to the whole: a sense, also, of growth, which is complementary to the sense of unity. It is as a developing situation that all your experience is unified. The unity is the unity of a story, a history.

Christian experience is all the above with the co-ordinating sense of unity and growth mysteriously intensified. In the experience of the fully mature Christian, there is a consuming certainty that his life and the whole of which his life is a part is a story being written by a personal God, whose personal nature is known and confessed *in* the meaning that he pours, moment by moment, into the whole of life. It is an intensely personal experience, and yet it is the reverse of private. Its very intensity and certainty preclude the uncertainty and agnosticism which must be present in a conviction that stops at the boundaries of one's own life. In any case, where are these boundaries? The consuming certainty that God is and is committed to me is the sense, in the very depths of the spirit, of his existence for all.

Now while we may describe in this way what Christian experience *is*, we do not thus account for its actually *working* in this world. The world is a tough place. It exerts colossal inertial pressures against a spirit which is the negation of inertia. It says 'You will die and I shall remain.' Doubtless the essentially shared and mutually enriching nature of the Christian experience makes it more than a match for the powers of darkness, but the experience of Christians has shown that this shared spirit has to adopt what might be called basic human survival techniques: the creation of symbols which, charged with the spirit, are able to store up its force 'against bad times'. The life of the totally committed is a rare phenomenon in the Christian body. Christians for the most part are distracted: they cannot bear, all the time, the burden of Christian consciousness. Against these unavoidable hazards and attenuations, the symbols are there, ever recalling the community to its true centre, ever available as a language able to be revitalized, as a meeting-place for divided hearts.

But the symbols, just because they are this world's way of securing human at-one-ness and continuity, have in them the seeds of death. Another consequence of their worldly provenance is that they tend to cluster into those massive wholes which we call cultures and which, when we are thinking in a temporal dimension, we call epochs. This clustering secures for the symbols a far greater permanence than they otherwise would have, but it also seals their doom. As they all came together in one precipitation, so they will all fall together when, for reasons that the people involved can never quite express, the attitudes that they enshrine cease to feel real and to convince. And this process is as irreversible as history itself.

Now the last full Christian constellation was medieval Christendom. We have to go back that far if we are to find a culture in which all that was known of man and his world was unified and centred in a consciousness of a divinely directed and significant history. As the Church moved out of that period she came under the necessity, on pain of losing her soul, of realizing anew in herself the sense of being the divine meaning of this world, of building up in herself the power that would *tend* to the creation of new symbols.

In this she did not and could not totally fail. But the symbols of the emergent Counter-Reformation church, and the symbols of the new churches, showed painfully by their mutual conflict that they no longer stood for the whole of man. And now that complicated period of digging-in has come to an end. There is, in the Church today, absolutely no set of symbols that speaks to the Christian heart in its world-situation and tells it that life here and now is the Resurrection. If anyone says 'But what about the Eucharist?' he misses the point and really proves the point. An enormous amount of world has to be shut out of the Church for the Eucharist to 'work', and this of course means that it does not work in the manner under consideration here.

Certainly it can be *asserted* and even firmly believed that the Resurrection is now and that now is the Resurrection. But do we not feel, even as we assert it, a certain powerlessness, a certain debility? We shall, for instance, be asked by many if not most Christians what on earth we mean. The more sympathetic will ask what 'exactly' we mean, and here we shall find ourselves too at a loss. The bare statement of meaningfulness has about it a weakness and vagueness that makes it at best a poor linguistic vehicle for passionate conviction. Since we hold this conviction we are necessarily groping for symbols, which alone give precision to *feeling*, and they are not to hand. It is very uncomfortable.

Worse, there is little awakening to this fact among theologians – even those of the 'progressive' variety. Indeed these latter conceal the disease by their enthusiasm, whereas the squares at least allow it to manifest itself.

There is in short not the necessary mechanism whereby the central Christian fact can declare itself today, can declare that it *is* today, that it is what today is. The whole available Christian vocabulary tends to put the Christian fact in the past. And when, in spite of this whole drift, it is still stoutly asserted that the Christian fact, in all its dimensions, *is* today, the question arises: what precisely is supposed to be happening, and where?

The answer given is that it is on a supernatural plane, in a dimension not available to experience. This is analogous to the decision of banks to issue paper money, tokens of a supply of bullion whose solid reality no longer figures in commerce. In the Church this is a desperate expedient. A 'supernatural' thus secured, never required to be shown, and therefore very difficult to share, must raise doubts as to its relevance and even its existence. This alarming breakdown is happening at this moment. The era opened by the Vatican Council has accelerated it, for history has always shown that revolutions only start when the ruling power starts easing up. And now the Church's 'supernatural credit' – meaning the supernatural *as* credit and no longer as world-changing fact – is in question. There is a run on the banks. The situation is aggravated by the fact that the people who tend to make the direct appeal to supernatural credit tend to be the people in authority. And when (as I think must happen in such a time as ours – there is no question of blame here) the disposition of affairs on the part of religious superiors betrays a certain agnosticism, loss of nerve, lack of daring and courage, a certain 'hoping for the best' as regards the results of their decisions about people – in short, a whole syndrome of symptoms that are the clean opposite of Paul's 'fruits of the Spirit' – the doubt as to the validity of 'the supernatural' to which they make constant appeal must deepen. It must be added however that those under authority in their turn must grow out of the immature habit of expecting the *superiors* to deliver the goods. For this too is the negation of the personal and communal nature of the Christian spirit.

A frequent escape-route is to say that the whole trouble is that we are growing soft, that a spot of persecution would soon awaken us to the present relevance of the Christian fact. Significantly the only type of persecution here envisaged is the standard type in which the martyr is given the choice between escaping execution and 'confessing Christ'. And this consideration does not further one whit the exploration into the power of Christ to give meaning to life today. There is no consideration given to a form of persecution which would bring us a little nearer the mark: that which expresses the active dislike of society for the live and active spirit that is impatient with its routines. It may well be that this type of persecution, which is at present *within* the Church rather than *of* the Church, will call forth the patient courage and charity of a real Christian conviction. The experience of being totally at loggerheads on the deepest things of life with people to whom we are bound in a common faith may be as creative as it is painful. It may even be the principal creative force in the Church at this moment. It is indeed creatively Christian to suffer the persecution of fellow Christians without the bitterness of party spirit, and to create for the prejudiced the space they require to widen their vision and to come to a generous affirmation of the flesh and in the flesh of reconciliation. And to be creatively Christian is to be about the creation of Christian symbols. This is the rebirth of love in the Christian community. It is in this love that the Christian affirmation of Christ now in the flesh and of the growing of a whole world towards God is lifted above the world of ideology and *Weltanschauung*, and becomes our true business as Christians.

It is fashionable to say that the essence of Christian faith is 'personal commitment to the Person of Jesus Christ'. I am trying to show here why that phrase, which is theologically sound, has today an inescapably sectarian ring, since it suggests, as well as commitment, a certain darkening of the mind, a methodical psychological exclusion of a mass of experience, a suspension. There is no escaping the erosion of Christian language, and no Christian thinking is worthy of the name that is not painfully conscious of this and addressed to its remedying.

There's got to be a new theology. Michel Quoist (cf. *Prayers of Life*, Gill, 1963) can go on till he's blue in the face rubbing our Christian noses in all the hideous human messes, asserting that a Christian confession that does not contain creative concern for people is no more than verbal. But we don't *really* believe what he says, because our theological structures do not allow this belief. Until our *theology* associates creatively God and you and me and this present moment of time and forbids us to think of any of these in isolation, we shall remain fundamentally paralysed and feel hope running out. The more we emphasize that the Christian thing is a corporate human flourishing in God, the more painfully evident it becomes that our concept of God will not support this burden of humanity. The heart, the centre of the Christian mind, is grown old and arthritic. The joy and bounce, the intellectual agility and adventurousness, have gone.

(Someone said the other day that the thing about the Greek theologians was that they obviously found God enormous *fun*. This is the sort of thing one 'doesn't say', and more's the pity. I've got more theology out of Arthur Dooley, who's always coming out with remarks of this kind, than from five years in the Roman schools. But if one makes this kind of remark and adds that we are dying of the Roman gravitas, people will say 'I agree, but surely you realize that we're bringing back the Greek Fathers?': and so, inexorably, the point is missed. It is a question not of reviving the Fathers but of waking up to a situation which no such revival can begin to rectify.)

If the centre, the God-concept, is left untouched, and we go on hammering the Quoist line, the love that is desired and required becomes purely moral, its only enthusiasm sentimental and humourless. Only when the basic theology is right can Christian love be seen to be and really felt to be the overflowing of the Christian fact. (Quoist surely is not balanced, and it is symptomatic of our problem that he is the best contemporary spiritual reading available.) We're tired of hearing what Christians *ought* to be like. We want to hear what a Christian *is* in relation to this present time. Going on and on about Christ everywhere, Christ looking through the eyes of the prostitute, Christ in the delinquent child, and leaving it at that, will not do. This identity between Christ and the human scene is only *part* of a total theological picture in which the extended Christ is the unfolding mystery of God. But try to make this work in the present theological picture where liturgists nervously feel for the right formulas and we are still trying to get the trinitarian tangles out of our hair, and see how the whole thing begins to creak. Fergus Kerr, O.P. (*New Blackfriars*, September 1965), has said that theology is a commentary on a contemporary experience of God – an experience not just in the theologian but of the epoch in which and for which he is writing. Can *any* living theologian say that that is what theology really is for him? Or even that he feels acutely ill at ease because theology is *not* that for him?

It is axiomatic that where basic theology is not healthy, i.e. supple, having bounce and humour, fervent Christian exhortation will be moralistic and sentimental. It will be forced to derive from within itself the fire that should be coming up from the core. It will be, consciously or unconsciously, in reaction against the theological structure that will not support it, and so trying to shift the centre of the Christian life from God to the restless heart of man. And thus we are now in a situation in which every worthwhile Christian movement is doomed to be unbalanced and to generate neurosis among its promoters. This situation will last until our notion of God recovers its sense of humour, its relatedness to the human whole.

The confrontation between even the best modern theology and people who really are *alive today* should make this point, even if undertaken simply as a sociological exercise. It would make the point rather brutally, for the precisions of the theologian would appear as unmistakably like the cautions of the socially insecure. Of course the nice old-style theologians wouldn't come off so badly in this venture. The very remoteness of what *they* have to say might even make them, in a piquant way, socially viable. It is the progressives who cheerfully take on the modern world in their small world who would come off worst. For they are trying to talk about the same things as the world. My recent contacts with a fairly wide spectrum of married people have made me sense acutely the basic ineptitude of so much avant-garde theological writing about married love.

Our present social revolution is throwing up, among other things, a class highly empowered by new money and considerable intelligence, in whom this vastly and suddenly increased scope makes painfully evident by contrast the lack of a real centre, a heart quickened to life. They are people who experience an immense amount of life and do not find life exciting. The heart, unable to grow to this situation, is instead stunned by it into a stunted and fearful state. In terms of such people it is not difficult to define the requirements for a valid God-concept. God is the excitement which life for these people does not have. Their conversion will require Christian witnesses whose overall characteristic is that they find life exciting. And in default of a new-minted God-concept, it is not possible to define the believer in God as one who finds life exciting. For a staid and fearful orthodoxy is at pains to keep 'God' distinct from the human flourishing that is nevertheless, according to real Christian orthodoxy, his most authentic manifestation in the flesh.

In conclusion I should like to single out what seems to me the most important proposition in this chapter and then to suggest that it is not as hopeless as it sounds. It is:

Christians who are conscious today are reduced, in default of symbols, to the bare assertion that Christ makes our life meaningful: and the bare statement of meaningfulness is, however emphatically made, a weak statement, simply because the language of meaningfulness is weak.

This is true. And if the proposition 'life is meaningful' has to do duty for the Christian affirmation today, we may as well sell out. But the point is that this proposition does *not* have such a portentous role. It is essentially something said by one Christian to another or to someone with whom he is 'in dialogue'. It does not draw attention to itself as a proposition but invites the other to become conscious of his life, of the things he is actually about, and to experience the shock of realizing that in fact he habitually religionizes, if he does religionize, and wonders about religion if he does not, in a way that does not directly evoke what *he* does and is from moment to moment. Given the fact that communication is vastly more than the words used, so that when the statement of meaningfulness is made, something of the unique vitality of the person making it may go over: and given the fact, which is not really different, that life in one can evoke life in another: and given the fact that God himself attends on the groping effort of a man to find meaning in his life: and given above all the fact that God in Christ has guaranteed this presence in a special and solemn way to the efforts of two or three gathered together to find him, it is not too much to see in the poor linguistic vehicle that is all Christians have in this lean but highly potential time, an instrument of Christian re-birth.

It is, in short, becoming daily more apparent that what is coming to be the only language Christians can use is a language that is only valid in a community context. The impoverishment of our language is in fact its becoming identical with the bare essence of language, which is the communication of man to man, life to life, heart to heart. Eventually this bare and basic commingling of lives issues triumphantly and ebulliently in art and symbol. But this it seems will be the happy experience of a future Christian age.

Note on the Phrase 'Commitment to the Person of Jesus Christ'

The attempt really to say what is *meant* by this phrase takes us through the whole gamut of human experience, heads towards the inbuilt human crisis, and arrives at an inclusive human reality, a human explosion into totality, that diverges sharply from the localized and contingent attachment which the phrase otherwise implies. We have to purge the Christian mind of its 'King over the water' fixation.

In principle the transition from Christ as memory to Christ as present fact takes place in the soul of each baptized person, in whom Christ dies and rises, and who dies and rises in Christ. The task is to make conscious this prodigious psychological revolution, to find for it a language. In such a language, the members of the Christian community, liberated from dug-in positions, surprised by joy, must needs love one another and grow together unto the perfect Man.

3

The Critique
of Woolwich

THE SITUATION OF PEOPLE TODAY VIS-À-VIS RE-
ligion is complex, featuring both the estrangement of people
from the Christian bodies, and the estrangement of the
Christian bodies from their true centre.

These two facts have clearly to be taken together if we are
to speak the authentic Christian word of our time. We cannot
set ourselves a two-stage programme: *first*, get Christians
to see what Christianity really is; *then* offer this renewed
Christianity to the world. For even committed Christians
today suffer the sense of irrelevance in religion.

The crucial question is: how much, or what part, of the
modern mind is potentially alive to the real demand of Christ,
to the encounter with God that is at the heart of life and not
in a specialized 'religious' activity?

Now in the proposed meet-up between an irreligious age
and the Christian non-religious encounter with God, the
latter partner must dominate. It is tempting to make the
obvious link-up, basing ourselves on what is, superficially,

a factor common to both parties, namely the 'non-religious' bit. This would mean saying something like this: 'You don't see much sense in religion. It seems to you that life's meaning and purpose is found in the relationships we form with each other. The more we rid these relationships of all selfishness, the closer we come to the meaning of life. Now that is what Christianity is "really" about. The Christian God is that "meaning", that "ultimate reality".'

This seems to me what the Bishop of Woolwich does. He has allowed the contemporary irrelevance of religion to be the dominant partner. He is using the Christian transcendence of religion not on its own humanly devastating terms, but as the corroboration of an approach that is in any case congenial to the modern mind. In this process the substance of the Christian Thing is lost, *not* because Woolwich's God is woolly as opposed to definite, religionless as opposed to religious, but because the disconcerting force of the Christian vision, its turning of this world inside out, its demand for a radical revolution at the hard core of man as the price of that vision, is not operative.

In reality, Christ displaces religion not because religion claims to put us in touch with a divine personal Being, but because it represents man's attempt to make sense of his life without unduly outraging his habitual way of thinking about himself and others and the world as a whole. In the religious world into which Christ came, this fixing of God as outside and sovereign *coincided* with this 'customary' and habitual or conventional way of thinking, and so the radical upsetting of man *coincided* with the dethronement of his God. But modern man's common sense does *not* settle in a religious pattern; so he's not going to be *un*settled by having the pattern destroyed, even by a bishop.

But I don't see at all clearly what Woolwich *ought* to have done. I realize now quite clearly that what I have written has been simply my attempt to make sense of God for myself. I came to the problem as a monk and a priest, saturated with monastic liturgy and Catholic theology. My rethinking has been focused round two preoccupations. First, the feeling that the problem of the love of God and the love of the brethren awaited a new and exciting solution in depth. Secondly, a feeling that the Cross evacuates 'religion', 'tears the God of this world out of the sky' so that 'the skies are clean and the only homage is life'. And both these working-points, not to speak of the exciting discovery of their inter-connection, could only *be* working-points for someone thoroughly trained by 'religion' – the religion of standard Catholic and monastic practice. So I lay myself open to the charge of doing what I said was not to be done, namely to get Christians to see *first*, before approaching the *further* task of 'speaking to our time'.

It would also seem that the working-out of a new God-concept is usefully addressed only to people who already *have* a God-concept, not merely as a vague memory from Sunday school but as the focus of some personal conviction and effort. To replace a God-concept that has never had any real meaning by a concept related to human experience amounts to little more than replacing Father Christmas by an awakening to the parental love that filled the stocking.

And yet I am reluctant to regard my efforts as directed exclusively to 'those within'. No one who is alive can possibly accept such a limited assignment.

The inspection of my two working-points discloses an interesting fact about them and about the way I went to work on them. The problem of love of God and love of neighbour may be an in-problem, but its solution takes us outside. For it became clear to me that the thing to think about is a very basic sense of unsatisfactoriness in our human relations, and that is not a specifically Christian experience. The Christian

may *state* it by saying he feels he is dividing his human relations from the love of God, but underlying this is or should
be the feeling of not being able to exist fully as himself *in*
those relationships. The feeling is not so much that our relationships have nothing to do with God, as that the self, to
which God for the Christian is the key, fails to be fully
realized in the community, in which however he obviously
should be fully realized. Here I reject the usual theistic account
which says: 'Of course the self is not fully realized in the
community: he needs God as well.' My answer to this is that
the customary, habitual confrontation of the self with the
community demands, if we are to have a full life, a radical
re-definition of self-in-community. To the Christian I then
say 'and this re-definition is of the regenerated man to whom
alone God is shown'. While to someone for whom 'God' is
meaningless I simply propose a re-definition of the self as the
condition of the full life. But in either case what I am saying
is that the self has to be redefined. My attack bears on an
oldness that has come upon our way of thinking of ourselves
and the others and the world. And this oldness is found
throughout the human community, whether it is graced with
the trappings of religion or bullied by the angry abstractions
of the left. The great cry we want to put up, the experience
to which we want to appeal, is *that it oughtn't to be like this*, it's
not *meant* to be like this. A cry that will be echoed in many
breasts, ranging from the averagely-placed curate in a pres-
bytery to the young sales executive in the average firm.
Somehow this cry has got to be got on to the same bearing
as the faith that tells of a human catastrophe and of liberation.
Something like this cry was being heard at the right depth
ten years ago, when we were told of a great new generation
that was engaged on a revolution too radically human to
accept the description political.

    Further analysis of this unsatisfactoriness in the community discovers in our tight and awkward relationships a closedness to the deeper springs of existence: more specifically the encapsulation of the ego from death, that death that links us with the whole cosmic process and suggests a common destiny: and about our indifference to *that*, there is something gigantically and dramatically wrong. And this leads me to reflect that my second working-point, the Cross, led me to the consideration of death, in terms of which the work was really done. And so here too I find the same pattern as with the first working-point: the aim was again one that only a religious person could have proposed, but its prosecution was not and could not be in religious terms.

It seems, in short, that the structure I have worked out for renewing the Christian understanding of God is also a structure that heads the human condition, as anyone experiences it, towards a need for a liberation altogether beyond the power of men to effect. So perhaps there is after all a way of thinking that at once makes the Christian ask again who God is, and the unbeliever begin to wonder whether such a being exists.

4

Christian
Poetry

WHY HASN'T THE SHEER POETRY OF THE CROSS BEEN
written? Is not all the Christian poetry that we have a poet-
izing of theology? Where – apart from the scripture – is the
poetry whence theology itself is born? Has the Cross ever
astonished people into poetry? Has it ever, in the soul of a
poet, torn down the whole world and rebuilt it? It would
be strange indeed if it hadn't. For the poet is above all the
man who *feels* what most people confusedly *know* they *are*:
feels the essential condition of man which is 'to be in the
world'. The poet travels freely in the Spirit across the boundaries that custom erects between man and the world. He
deconventionalizes those boundaries, and flows into the world
and back into himself to find the world there. He celebrates
the primordial nuptials of the world and the self. Out of this
celebration he creates gods. He reminds the philosopher that
however strongly the latter asserts the transcendence and
originality of God there cannot be a fully human feeling for
God as transcendent. In so far as he is a man living in the

world the philosopher is bound to *mean* by God, at least in part, what the poet means.

The poet's search for the living and true God is different from the philosopher's. For while the philosopher simply *corrects* the finitude that God assumes when man tries to realize him, the poet builds up an ambivalent and ironic attitude to the God of this world. He will play in a thousand moods the triangle of self, world, and God. Our reason for expecting the Cross to have touched the poet is that the Cross enters this pattern to alter it totally and finally. It dethrones the God of this world, not as does the philosopher by a stroke of the pen that leaves the world unchanged and still requiring its God, but in such a way as to establish the living and true God in this world of man.

The Cross races slow man to his conclusion. It concludes the love-play between the self and the world, which accords to a presiding deity alternatively reverence and ribaldry: for it consummates the love-play in death, and in this now unequivocal relationship the living God declares himself unequivocally. The Cross does not end the fun, as said Swinburne. It does not merely give a deeper dimension to the fun, as says the Christian humanist. It *consummates* the fun in a perpetual astonishment of man that is Revelation. It is of this perpetual astonishment, this stunning into life, that one would have expected a rather amazing poetry to be born.

Properly the Cross throws the poet right off his bearings in his attempt to write religious poetry about it. It should throw him back into the human and into the world, which is now no longer the place of the godless phase of the pagan exultation in life, but the place of an exultation in life that is, in a new and exciting sense, worship. And somehow this does not seem to have happened, except sometimes in the New Testament. Paul's Hymn to Love is just such an exultation, a joyous exercise of the human spirit in its new-found freedom, reaching beyond good and evil and life and death.

The Cross seems to have been *divided*, between the theologians, who have elaborated its implications but lost its anthropological impact, and the poets, who have welcomed it as a glorious addition to their world of gods. Indeed it seems that the very divinity of this Hero (learned from the theologians) has, far from desacralizing the universe, crowned the pagan soul with a uniquely potent trophy.

Somehow or other the *man* in the Christ affair has got lost. I mean the man that in Christ stands before the Father with the gaiety of transformed flesh and the freedom of the universe. He has been *divided* into the *special* man who underwent the experience of Cross and Resurrection, and the rest of men whom a sort of pagan reverence has prevented from feeling in their flesh and blood and bones the sacrament of the new man. And it is from this man who has got lost, and from him alone, that the dangerous poetry of the Cross is to be born.

In this context I wonder whether we do not need a quite new history of heresy. Such a history would show how the wild and lyric element in the Christian vision has not so far been able to be contained within the orthodox Christian body but has been forced out, partly through its own lack of maturity and charity and partly through a lack of maturity and charity in the Church. We must surely look forward to, and strive towards, a new maturity in the Church, wherein the antithesis between orthodoxy and enthusiasm may be transcended. And this is to look forward to a new poetry of the Cross. We want something a lot better than the Cross that the theologians have theologized and that the poets have jewelled. We seek the new language that shall get the Cross in focus. It feels like it's never been really in focus. This is to some extent an optical illusion, due to our inability to get *past Christian epochs* perfectly in focus. But I'm convinced it's not only that.

The Cross in the Christian epochs necessarily created its own unique category in the genus 'event.' The uniqueness consists in the connecting of universal religious significance with a particular brutally historical event. But the tendency has been merely to *assert* this connection and leave it to the soul to get on with it. The result is that the soul feels *passive* to an astounding assertion, whereas it should feel liberated, painfully understood, shot out into the dark world to grow there, newly recognizing, feeling for new words. Instead, the Cross has merely *surprised* the soul, not surprised it by joy. There should have been born a Christian exultation in new life. Limiting itself to the sheer assertion of the connection, the Christian mind has limited itself to paradox, and a paradox is a paradox is a paradox.

The point is that the Cross has not declared its reality to the heart of man. The supposition has been that God made this new category of significant event *out of the religious materials* provided by mankind. But he didn't. He made it out of *man*. He made it out of this tortured and dreaming parcel of flesh and blood, whose very yearning makes him dissatisfied with 'religion', whose affair with this world goes far deeper than religion is ever able to cope with, whose hunger for God drives him *through* that affair whereas religion tends to draw him back from it.

The focus is at the centre of a man's being, where death speaks to him and says 'You should know me, you know, for I am you.' In that dark knowing place the crucified is a blinding light in which God declares himself in a destruction of gods on a scale and at a depth that man dare not attempt. Whereas the frustrated virginal Christian soul has to go to Wagner to indulge, guiltily, its dream of Götterdämmerung.

5

In a Word

HUMAN LIVING AS IT IS NORMALLY PURSUED IS AN
escape from reality. The gospel message is a recall to reality,
revealed as a mystery of forgiveness. It is an appeal to man
on the vast and portentous scale of his historical self-build-up
to take another way and discover himself for the first time.
It is an appeal to man who builds against death to realize
that in doing so he hardens his heart. In building against
death, man distorts himself. Quite naturally he divides life
up sharply into the part that he can do something about and
the part he can do nothing about. The latter part is death.
And thus death, which man must know to be his one certain
future and therefore a prime ingredient in his self-understanding and real living, becomes for the social builder
something to be disguised and disregarded. So the great
human edifice goes up with time on its side and death as its
unavowed underside. History is a vast papering over of the
human crack.

But man is too wise and tender to commit his destiny
entirely to the social builder. That is to say, he requires a
more realistic look at his death than the social builder will

allow him. And so he calls to his aid philosophy, religion, the arts – all the things that 'humanize'. Between all these and the practical concern of man the builder, there grows up a relationship of enormous complexity, about which all that can be said is that it has no finality.

If we may risk a generalization of this vastly complicated human phenomenon, let us say that human life is, through and through, a compromise. Who would dare quarrel with such a venerable cliché! Man takes a half-look at the dark unmanageable side of his life, to derive therefrom enough reality to carry on, but not enough to – well, what? A bloody good question.

The more one lets that one sink in the more one sees that if man distorts himself by only half-recognizing death, he would equally distort himself were he to accord to that enigmatic fact full recognition. A society that became convinced by death would soon become bound by it and become extinct. It would lose the heart which nevertheless it cannot find in the world of its building.

The whole effort of theology now must be to state, in this prepared anthropological context, *how* Christ mounts the Cross and so makes his transforming statement in the flesh: to relate the shocking naïveté of the Cross to the whole démarche of human culture, in such a way that the latter is not invalidated but simply shown to be less than fully human. Our theology must show the crucified as that heart which society seeks and betrays in its necessary building of the human whole. Crucified and declared in the power of the Spirit, Christ is shockingly man in the midst of all that men do and make of themselves. The human whole as men achieve it, the hard enduring institution, claims its victims, and Christ indeed joins himself to their number. And yet he sounds in that victimhood a note never heard before and, once heard, never again to be silenced. For here, unanswerably, *is*

184 · GOD IS A NEW LANGUAGE

the human whole where mortal man must perforce recognize and find himself. Here is the human polity, the common life, and not the despair of those things – those very things that formerly depended on the human city for which the heart is expendable.

And the human whole thus undeniably asserted, the man thus enacted without pretence or compromise in the whole gamut of his living and dying, is, without further explanation, the place of faith. Here the naked encounter with that final reality that men call God but know and are known of only as the nails are driven into history.